STORM
in a
FLOWER VASE

by Anton Burge

STORM IN A FLOWER VASE

by Anton Burge

First performed at the Arts Theatre, London, on 13th September, 2013, with the following cast:

CONSTANCE SPRY (Connie)	Penny Downie
HANNAH GLUCKSTEIN (Gluck)	Carolyn Backhouse
HENRY SPRY (Shav)	Christopher Ravenscroft
SYRIE MAUGHAM	Carole Royle
ROSEMARY HUME	Sheila Ruskin
VAL PIRIE	Sally George

Understudies

ALL FEMALE ROLES	Yvonne Riley
HENRY SPRY	Keith Myers

Production Team

DIRECTOR	Alan Strachan
DESIGNER	Morgan Large
LIGHTING	James Whiteside
SOUND	Mark Dunne
PROJECTION	Duncan Mclean
CASTING	Kate Plantin CDG
PRODUCTION MANAGER	Tim Higham
COMPANY STAGE MANAGER	Phillip Hussey
ASM INTERN	Chris Smythe
PROPS SUPERVISOR	Mig Kimpton
PRODUCTION FLORIST	Stephen Wicks
COSTUME SUPERVISOR	Tracy Styles
WIGS AND MAKEUP SUPERVISOR	Diana Estrada
PRODUCER	Ann Pinnington
ASSOCIATE PRODUCER	Mig Kimpton
GENERAL MANAGER	Chris Corner
MARKETING	Will Maidwell and Frankie Barber for EMG
PRESS	Cliona Roberts at CRPR

ANTON BURGE

Actor and writer Anton Burge has written eight plays for women, all focusing on the lives of celebrated women of the 19th and 20th centuries, including *Whatever Happened to the Cotton Dress Girl?*, *G & I* (both New End Theatre, Hampstead), *Bette & Joan* (Arts Theatre, UK tour and a Broadway production is planned for next year), and the forthcoming *Lady Mosley's Suite* and *Gung Ho Gertie!* He is also the author of a forthcoming book *Portraying Elizabeth*, a study of actresses' interpretations of Elizabeth I, from Sarah Bernhardt to the present day.

THANKS

The author would like to thank Ann Pinnington, Stephen Wicks, Deborah Smith, Alan Strachan, Emily Hayward, Sue Shephard and Katie Langridge.

AUTHOR'S NOTES

A note on the sets:

All sets are implied by props, sound and lighting. Sets must be changed with speed and the minimum of fuss: the actors themselves can do many of these as they enter and leave the scene. A curtain may also be used as part of a set, to disguise another behind it. The set could have the effect of the shop in places: Objet and pedestals with floral designs upon them and much of the sets are supposed or, as in Act 1 Scene 9, imagined.

A note on the lighting:

Throughout the play there should be a continual battle of colour with white. The opening sequence, gradually submerge into the brilliant white of a Syrie Maugham interior. As the relationship between Constance and Gluck deepens, so the colour dilutes; as the relationship falls apart so Syrie's white influence dismantles and colour once again begins to dominate.

A note on Constance:

The actress playing Constance remains on stage throughout most of the play, unless stated in the text, i.e. Act 1 Scene 2 and top of Act 1 Scene 10. Therefore many costume changes etc. will be made on stage; these are chiefly done by under dressing or the adding of certain props, makeup etc. These moments alone should be moments of intimacy with the audience, where they see Constance solitary, often vulnerable, and private: touching up her make up with her compact, coming to terms with what has happened in the last scene.

The action of the play, with the exception of one scene in Act Two which is set in Cornwall, takes place in London between 1932 and 1936.

The play is dedicated to the memory of Lucia (Lulu)

ONE

Spring 1932 is projected across the stage. Music fades. Floral images in the vein of Constance Spry's work of the early 1930s are shown as if by photographic slides. The emphasis is on the mixing of colours. Dust particles fill the air and the noise of the projector buzzes. The floral images are all in black and white. The slide rests upon a display of hyacinths, ranunculus and anemones. A bright, coloured gel illuminates the image. Constance Spry, 50s, steps out onto the stage, in front of the large image. She shields her eyes a little from the light. She wears a rather tweedy, though smart, skirt and jacket, with a pullover underneath. She is neat and well dressed throughout. She has an attractive, twinkling quality and easy charm. She has great enthusiasm which outweighs her sometimes lacking confidence. She holds some well worn notes, which she refers to; her spectacles; and a small nosegay of the flowers in the picture. She wears a four strand rope of pearls throughout the play. She has a firm, yet quiet manner. Her voice is decidedly upper class, though dips on occasion into something resembling a Midlands accent.

CONSTANCE

I feel nervous—it has been such a long time since I spoke in front of an audience, Shav.

A dim relief on Shav, 50s, standing at the side of the stage, watching his wife.

SHAV

You don't have to do it, you know.

CONSTANCE

Oh, but I want to. It's just the last time I spoke about flowers was to a class of under sevens. *(She looks at her notes.)* And you do think colour is a good place to start?

SHAV

Go on. Colour.

CONSTANCE

(Referring to her notes) Colour, yes. Thank you, Shav. I suppose people will be interested?

SHAV

Just remember you have been asked to give this talk.

CONSTANCE

I know, but that doesn't make it any easier faced with row upon row of expectant faces.

SHAV

You were a teacher for God's sake!

CONSTANCE

Thank you, Shav, but this is hardly the same thing. But I will do my best and try to think of the ladies of the Flower Guild as a class of under sevens! *(She clears her throat and begins, falteringly, reading from her notes.)* It has been my great privilege, these last three years, to run 'Flower Decorations' in London, after spending my time working for the Red Cross, then as a welfare supervisor and then as a teacher and headmistress. *(She stops and looks to Shav.)* You've gone very quiet.

SHAV

I was listening! Now go on. Isn't it something about when you were young?

CONSTANCE

(Looking at her notes, turning a page) But I always held on to the memory of the girl who spent her pocket money on flower seeds. So, *(Gesturing to the wings)* with the aid of my dear husband—

SHAV

Just husband will do.

CONSTANCE

—husband, I have been fortunate enough to express my enduring love of flowers and views on floristry—

SHAV

Not floristry—flower decoration. Floristry is a trade.

CONSTANCE

—on flower decoration, and hopefully this afternoon, with the help of these slides— *(She looks at the most recent flower image.)* — and the benefit of a little knowledge, we may go hand in hand and appreciate flowers, old and new, and even some things that we had not considered for use in our homes.

SHAV

Find a better word for things.

CONSTANCE

Sorry. Shall I jump to 'Colour in the Home'?

SHAV

I would. I thought that was what you wanted me to hear?

CONSTANCE

I was running into it.

SHAV

Well, make a dash for it instead!

CONSTANCE

Thank you, Shav. Very well. *(She holds up the display.)* Take this vibrant display of early spring blooms. One might say the reds and blues and purples are too much, too strong to compete in the same vase—

SHAV

Can't you find a proper vase?

CONSTANCE

No! That is the whole point of it. Not everyone will have a vase, but they will own a pickle jar.

SHAV

But it's the Ladies Flower Guild!

CONSTANCE

Just let me run on, I've made some changes: *(She quickly checks her notes.)* But be brave, ladies, and don't let the tame wind of mediocrity influence your choices for the decoration of your home!

(To Shav) I think that works? *(Refers to her notes)* For in the right context, and with the correct accompaniment, every flower, like everybody, has its place. Flowers for everyone!

SHAV

All good so far.

CONSTANCE

Thank you. Many years ago, when I was quite a young woman, I had a journey to work that was dreary to say the least. To enliven the trip, I gathered each morning flowers from my small garden to disperse along the way: a violet for the ticket collector, a wallflower for the bus conductor—

SHAV

Keep to the point. The ladies will want instruction, not reminiscences.

CONSTANCE

Oh, I thought they might appreciate that. *(Referring to notes. The light gradually closes in on her. Shav is soon in darkness.)* I see, yes... *(In time, as her confidence grows, the notes in her hand fall to her side. To her audience)* So today's talk is a look at the breaking down of barriers that flowers can bring about; the purging of ourselves, of shyness that can hold us back in our friendships, simply achieved by the giving of a flower, and the unlikely bedfellows we may bring from the garden into the house. I am not trying to persuade, but merely to make you aware, so that you don't miss out on anything!

Well, Shav, what do you think?

Music. Lights fade

TWO

Music fades. Images of London in the early 1930s. **The Spry Residence, London** *is projected across the stage. Lights up on an indication of the interior of Henry 'Shav' Spry's London study. A masculine, shabby room.* SHAV: *untidily dressed, tall, handsome, attends to paperwork at his desk. He rises and goes to the window. The sound of London, as a taxi pulls up. Sounds of doors, muffled voices, money exchanged etc. Smoothing down his hair, he looks at his watch and sighs. Voices off: Servant and* VAL. *The door swings open:* VAL *Pirie enters: harsh, made up face; dressed in an unflattering summer suit, early 40s, she carries a bunch of foxgloves, wrapped in paper.*

VAL

Lord, I thought I should never get away.

SHAV

(Rising) On time as usual. Just wrong day.

VAL

Does it matter?

> *She laughs knowingly as he makes to kiss her, crushing some of the foxgloves in the process.*

Careful, Shav, you'll ruin them. And don't let them touch your skin or you'll get a nasty rash, and you know what that can be like!

8

SHAV

(Laughing) Really! And to what do I owe the honour of your visit? We don't have long.

> *Freeing herself, she casts off her hat and places the wrap of flowers on the desk, disturbing his work.*

VAL

Trying as ever, forever trying to balance the books and keep the creditors from the door!

I thought you might have an urge to see me, that's all.

SHAV

I see.

VAL

Really, Shav, it's becoming quite impossible what with—

SHAV

No scenes. Please.

> *He moves closer to her, knocking the flowers.*

VAL

Careful! Don't you read the mystery writers? Digitalis in the salad! Was it Cook's fault or was it really an accident? Did Gladys the maid pick them thinking it was sorrel?

SHAV

What nonsense you talk.

VAL

It isn't nonsense. Mrs. Christie rakes in a fortune with her murder mysteries. I bet if I could churn them out like sausage as she does, you might be more appreciative of me!

SHAV

I am. I'm sure you think that sitting here in my counting house, watching the coffers grow, is my only pleasure in life.

VAL

Well isn't it?

SHAV

Certainly not. I have my travels abroad, I have my time in Scotland,
I have...

VAL

Well, I think you should look to those coffers. We really do need to
make some changes to the way things are run at the shop. The girls
for instance! We can't be forever relying on goodwill and cream
buns to sustain them through the day. They put up with it because
they worship her, I can't think why.

SHAV

Careful.

VAL

Yes, yes, but the Horse, for example, is she really necessary? And
these actors forever coming and going—

SHAV

Aesthetes you mean!

VAL

She adores them; they make her laugh.

SHAV

Surely we can do better than that. There are people crying out for
jobs.

VAL

Ah! I see you agree with me. At last!

SHAV

I never said I didn't.

VAL

Well your loyalty might have been split.

SHAV

It has to be.

I do see, though, that there are problems to overcome, but you must admit that the business has come a long way in such a short space of time. Why, it seems only yesterday she was decorating Atkinson's Perfumery 's window. Police had to move the crowds on! I was so proud of her.

VAL

I know, I know, and "so was London!"

And since then the telephone hasn't stopped ringing.

And I bet you hadn't banked on that? Didn't expect it to become an empire in such a short space of time. An empire bearing your name: Constance Spry, Flower Decorations.

SHAV

As you well know, I wasn't expecting anything of the sort, and would have been perfectly content for her to continue doing the flowers for her society friends, as a gesture of goodwill.

VAL

So as not to neglect her beloved husband!

SHAV

You know that isn't part of Connie's and my... arrangement.

> *He tries to hold her. She moves quickly, looking at the pictures on the wall, buying time.*

VAL

We had John Gielgud in the other day looking for work for his sister. I ask you. What can she know about floristry?

SHAV

Flower decoration. Floristry is a trade.

VAL

The Horse said that perhaps if Nell Gielgud was no good with flowers she could help me with the books in the office!

SHAV

Is she pretty this Nell Gielgud?

VAL

(Warily) Very.

SHAV

Then she would be an asset to the shop, but I don't need her working alongside you, Val.

VAL

Is she to be the next of your conquests I wonder?

SHAV .

(Looking very seriously at her) Whatever do you mean? I don't want her getting in the way of us. That is what I mean.

> *She moves away from him and deftly lights a cigarette from her case.*

VAL

You want so much.

> *A beat. They look at each other. She circles him.*

So, have you missed me?

SHAV

Of course, my dear. *(He looks at her.)*

VAL

I know, I know, I shouldn't be here. She could return and we would have to think of an excuse!

SHAV

(Smiling. getting close to her) Anyway, I thought that it was I, not you, that was the instructor on such matters?

> *He takes the cigarette from her lips, she snaps at his fingers, he then goes to the window and tosses it into the street, leaving the sash up.*

SHAV

You know the rules, Val.

VAL

Of course. I know the rules: you run the business, and nothing must get in the way of the business. Just be aware that I have a continuing role to play in that business.

SHAV

(He moves towards her and finally embraces her.) I am well aware of that, my dear. You are admired and feared in equal measure. You are my ears and eyes and I depend upon you more than you know.

That is why I don't want Little Nell from the theatre bothering you.

And that is why you must stay doing what you are doing and how you are doing it. Can you imagine if some halfwit chorus girl started helping you with the accounts? She would soon get wind that something was going on between the boss and Miss Val, while the other boss was doing the flowers!

He releases her.

VAL

(Looking towards the window) Ah, the breeze will come in and rid the memory of me.

SHAV

Not at all. *(He pushes down the window, leaving it slightly ajar.)*

VAL

Not completely: see—there is a gap, very fine, but there is a gap. In time the memory of me will trickle through it, like water running out of a chipped vase.

SHAV

No there isn't, there is no gap, no chip as you say.

VAL

(She slams the window shut.) There!

The clock strikes seven.

SHAV

You know the rules. If Connie isn't working late, as she isn't today, you shouldn't be here.

VAL

So, why won't you act on my findings? *(Pulling out a bill)* Here, look: Atikinsons' weekly window, charged at £5! And if she thinks it needs it, she shoves in another flower, without even adding it to the bill! And Heals windows a mere £1. Can you credit it? £1!

SHAV

(At last taking a slip of paper) Let me see.

VAL

She has no business sense.

SHAV

Well if that is the case, neither have I. Is that what you're saying?

VAL

And look at this: Price 30 shillings, cost of the flowers 42 shillings. Saying nothing about my time.

> SHAV *takes this slip and reads it.*

This shouldn't be happening, Shav. For God's sake, you're a trained chartered accountant!

SHAV

(Sitting. after a moment, sadly) I wanted her to be happy.

VAL

You wanted her out of the way you mean.

SHAV

Thank you, Val. Come along now, get your things...

> *He collects up the flowers for her, motioning her out.*

VAL

She's not stupid. Something will happen, I know it will!

Fortunately I imagine she has enough secrets of her own to excuse other people's.

SHAV

What do you mean?

VAL

Just that. We all have secrets.

He goes to the door.

(Hurriedly) They're planning a cookbook. Did you know? The Horse and she. Baking tins won't actually be swimming in branches and catkins for a change. And gravy boats will be used for gravy. Didn't you know that, Shav?

Maybe it will be a good thing? Fill the coffers, God knows the business needs it, and I admit people do buy her flower books, they seem to lap up putting daisies in their milk jugs.

SHAV

Don't make fun of her, Val.

VAL

The Horse is behind it, you realize that? Wants to see her ugly name in print. Hume: sounds like a throat lozenge.

(At the door) I just hope it won't have that receipt/recipe for that curried muck she gave us for lunch the other day!

SHAV

Oh, shut up!

VAL

Strange how it slipped your mind to mention the book to me. You will let me know about it, won't you?

Shav nods.

VAL *(cont.)*

Make sure that I play a part; my name would look much prettier on the cover.

SHAV

Goodnight Miss Pirie. See you *tomorrow* with the receipts, and please try and stick to our allotted times in the future.

VAL

Call me later? Even if it is only to say "Goodnight".

SHAV

I always do, don't I? Let me kiss you.

VAL

Why?

SHAV

Because I deserve it for the battering you have just given me.

> *But she exits, banging the door.*

(Downing his drink) Bloody bitch!

> *Music.* SHAV *pours himself another drink and begins to look at the invoices.*

> *Fade, the time passes.*

THREE

Downstage an indication of the hall of the Sprys' London house. CONSTANCE *enters carrying a mass of white flowers: anthuriums, amaryllis, arums, tulips etc. Her handbag is hanging from her arm, a roll of brown paper under her other arm and an unusual white marble container dangling precariously from her fingertips. The latch key is held between her teeth. She wears a light suit and hat, and is followed by a tall 'horse'-like woman laden down with containers:* ROSEMARY, *late 50s, wearing a dark dress. As they talk they sort the items. Music fades.*

CONSTANCE

Lord, I thought we'd never get away! And the heat! London at the moment—well, it gets worse, doesn't it?

She relieves herself of the items. In time she will put the flowers in the bucket.

ROSEMARY

Where shall I put these?

CONSTANCE

I long for a weekend in the country again.

Oh, anywhere, Rosemary—pop them on the floor for the time being and then you must run along.

ROSEMARY

(Putting them down and admiring them) I think these will work well. Once they've been scrubbed and painted. I don't mind, you know that. I like to help.

CONSTANCE

I know, I know, dear. And I don't know what I should do without you, what with your tact and your—

ROSEMARY

Oh please, now, Connie.

CONSTANCE

No, I mean it. But you have a life too. And it's an early morning again at the flower market for you if I'm to get up to— *(She pauses a moment, sniffing.)* I really mean it though, I don't know— *(She breaks off, sniffing.)*

ROSEMARY

Thank you. *(Looking at the vases again)* Yes, I do like them. You were right of course.

CONSTANCE

While they're here, I might try one in Shav's dressing room, it needs something, just a focal point to dilute the brown... and they won't put any flowers in the shade will they?

ROSEMARY

But after tomorrow you can, can't you? Pop to the country, to Park Gate?

What's the matter?

CONSTANCE

(Sniffing. Distracted) Shav is heading down with Val, to work on the books or something... She wants to know more about the business side of things.

Though if it is anything like last time, they'll be in the woods collecting foliage, and coming back with very little.

I suppose I will join them.

ROSEMARY

(Embarrassed. Picking up the marble vase) What is this one for?

CONSTANCE

Oh that. That's for that job tomorrow in Hampstead.

I do think her skill is in running things, don't you? So she must know more about the business side of things. And I can't teach her.

ROSEMARY

(Cautiously) If it will keep her away from the customers and off the girls' backs, it can't be a bad thing. I don't think she has a natural bent for flower decoration do you?

CONSTANCE

(Laughing) We couldn't do without her though. I have to face that. Not like you of course, but she does have a... well, a way about her.

ROSEMARY

Well, I wouldn't go that far. And why couldn't you do without her?

CONSTANCE

Well, well... she is very good at her job, you must admit that.

ROSEMARY

She takes the pressure off you, you mean?

    Constance looks at her.

CONSTANCE

You mean at the shop? *(Removing her hat, her back to Rosemary. She sniffs again.)*

ROSEMARY

Why do you keep sniffing?

CONSTANCE

Can you smell her?

ROSEMARY

Who? Smell wh—What do you mean? *(She also sniffs.)*

CONSTANCE

She's been here.

ROSEMARY

You mean Val?

CONSTANCE

(Quickly) Of course, of course I mean her.

She said that she wouldn't be popping by, nothing to bring, it could wait for Friday; but she came, didn't she?

ROSEMARY

Well, you can't be sure Connie...

CONSTANCE

Of course I can. It's a hard smell, that scent she wears, not like any flower I've ever worked with.

ROSEMARY

(After a moment. Concerned) Why don't you sit down a moment? Everything is done. You've been overdoing it. You know I don't know how you keep at it, all hours, like you do.

Your feet will be playing up again.

> Constance sits and kicks off her shoes.

Better?

CONSTANCE

(She nods.) Yes, thank you. *(She then becomes upset.)*

ROSEMARY

Oh Connie!

CONSTANCE

(Pretending nothing has happened) No, no I'm quite alright. Quite alright.

ROSEMARY

You say she isn't a problem but...

CONSTANCE

(*Wiping her eyes and blowing her nose*) You know Rosemary, sometimes it is absolutely fine and I can manage it all, but other times, well, something throws me off kilter, like that damned scent, and it's as if the display just won't behave. The flowers won't sit suitably. The effect is beyond my control!

ROSEMARY

Sometimes it is better to turn a blind eye where men are concerned.

CONSTANCE

You think? Well, that must be it.

> *Rosemary nods.*

Part of me wishes I knew nothing about it, and part of me is happy that my time is my own in so many ways, but that scent, well that scent. It just isn't feminine is it? And one does like to be thought of as feminine still. And I know they correspond. Letters.

> *Rosemary puts a hand on Constance's arm.*

CONSTANCE (*cont.*)

Did you know?

ROSEMARY

I—I had sensed something...

CONSTANCE

Of course you knew. Oh, I'm sorry, I shouldn't have said anything. Always better not to. Do you think the staff know? You know what girls are.

ROSEMARY

I doubt it, they all take what she says with a pinch of salt. Terrified of her. You know they won't speak out, otherwise they would have formed a committee against the lavatory that doesn't flush properly, the kitchen that isn't sanitary, and Miss Pirie who isn't nice!

CONSTANCE

(*Laughing*) Stop! Stop!

ROSEMARY
(Smiling) There, that's better.

CONSTANCE
(Picking up a pot to look at) Well, I suppose he has his needs, but she seems the more cavalier of the two, wouldn't you say?

But then what has she got to lose?

ROSEMARY
(Incredulous) Oh Connie, don't be silly! Her job of course!

SHAV *enters, dressed as before.*

SHAV
What's this? Good heavens! Connie sitting down! Well I never! *(Joking, slightly uneasy with the dependable and efficient Rosemary.)* Hello, Rosemary. How was today at the factory?

ROSEMARY
(Laughing politely) All fine, thank you Shav.

I ought to be getting along actually, while it's still light...

SHAV
Good, good.

How are you, Connie? Everything alright? Feet again?

CONSTANCE
(She rises and kisses him lightly. Over the next few speeches she moves quickly on and off stage carrying her pots etc. minus her shoes.) That's right. *(To Rosemary)* You run along home, Rosemary. I've kept you long enough. *(To Shav)* What a day! It's been silly, plain silly, hasn't it? She'll tell you. And we really must get that shop lavatory fixed, Shav!

ROSEMARY
You sure you don't need any more help?

SHAV
Yes, yes, a hand? *(Though he actually doesn't do anything)* And how much will that cost?

CONSTANCE

(Bustling about. To Rosemary) No, no, certainly not darling, you run along home! I won't take advantage! She's done quite enough, Shav—make her go!

SHAV

(To Rosemary) You've had your orders!

CONSTANCE

(Entering again) We didn't even have time for our sit down after the market, did we? The shop was a bun fight! Deckchairs just stared at us longingly, at the back of the shop. Tell him.

SHAV

Deckchairs?

CONSTANCE

(Continuing in and out. To herself, bringing the flowers back in) On second thoughts I think I'll leave these by the door, it'll be cooler. I don't want them too open.

ROSEMARY

I snipped the ends again before we left today, so they should have a good drink over night.

CONSTANCE

Thank you, dear. *(Then to Shav)* Oh, the deckchairs, I didn't tell you, did I? Yes! It was Rosemary's idea. It's a heavenly idea—tell him, dear. They're so comfy for a moment's zzzz, at the back of the shop, after the flower market, but not today! And the telephone, tell him, it never stopped, I felt like cutting the cable! We did a marvellous display for Lady Ribblesdale's lunch though: all flame coloured azaleas and brilliant delphiniums in bowls.

SHAV

Such vigorous colours, what would the mock virgin of white say?

CONSTANCE

Well it can't be white all the time, can it? I thought they looked very suitable together. And don't laugh at Syrie like that.

SHAV

I stand corrected. Though there has been a rumour that she has pickled so much furniture of late, she's going to pickle her own coffin! *(He laughs.)*

Nobody else laughs.

She has an unshakeable belief in her own talents, that woman.

CONSTANCE

As have I! We have to! *(To Rosemary)* Now why are you still here?

ROSEMARY

See you when you get back from Hampstead then.

CONSTANCE

Hold a deckchair for me!

ROSEMARY

I will! *(Taking Constance's hand)* And you are sure—

CONSTANCE

(Releasing her hand) Perfectly, you run along.

Rosemary makes for the door.

CONSTANCE *(cont.)*

I'll come straight to the shop. It shouldn't take too long. I know the sort of thing Prudence would like to give as a gift.

(To Shav) See Rosemary out will you?

SHAV

(Gesturing) But the door is only through there.

ROSEMARY

(Exiting) I'm fine, really.

He sees Rosemary out. Constance stares at the bucket of white flowers at her feet. Shav returns with a letter.

CONSTANCE

Evening post? Something for me?

SHAV

No, afraid not. Something for me. *(Exiting with the unopened letter)* I'll see you at dinner. And then we need to go through some accounts.

CONSTANCE

(Her back to him) Whatever for?

SHAV

Well, I had thought that as things seem to be developing so quickly, well, we might take a look... together.

> *She turns. They look at each other.*

No?

CONSTANCE

Things do seem to be developing rather. But I really need time to focus on doing the flowers.

You know I can't cope with all of... that.

SHAV

As you wish.

> *Shav makes to leave, then hesitates.*

CONSTANCE

(Smiling) How was Val?

SHAV

Val?

CONSTANCE

Yes. Val.

SHAV

Fine. She was fine.

CONSTANCE

(Attending to the flowers) Good.

Shav exits. Constance stands up straight, watching him retreat, sighs. The light fades, closing in on the bucket of white flowers. Music. As the scene changes, Constance removes her jacket and adds an overall to her costume; she continues to wear her hat. Some light remains upon her.

FOUR

Music fades. Images of Hampstead, early 1930s. A reception room at Hannah Gluckstein's home. Projection reads: **Bolton House, Hampstead**. *Lights up on another part of the stage. Constance arranging the white flowers, laid out in a box on a card table. In the marble vase, positioned on a pedestal, is the 'Alba' arrangement, nearly finished. She still wears her hat. She works for some moments before Hannah (Gluck) enters. She is in her late 40s, tall, thin and masculine, dressed in men's clothes and an artist's smock, open, revealing a man's waistcoat and shirt and tie. She smokes a cigarette. She watches Constance at work. After a moment she comes forward. Constance drops some of the flowers. It is apparent that Gluck was expecting someone grander than Constance.*

CONSTANCE

Oh good heavens! Foolish of me.

GLUCK

Not at all. I startled you. *(Holding out her hand)* How do you do? I am Gluck. *(As in "Duck")*

CONSTANCE

Oh how do you do? I'm Constance Spry.

GLUCK

You're Constance Spry?

CONSTANCE

Yes, I do hope I didn't disturb you Miss Gluck. Your maid said you were painting and must have complete silence.

GLUCK

The famous Mrs. Spry of whom society speaks. I am honoured that you have come all this way yourself to employ Prudence's gift. I didn't realize that you implemented commissions yourself.

CONSTANCE

Oh yes, yes, I do. When I can, Miss Gluck.

GLUCK

I must correct you. It is Gluck.

CONSTANCE

I beg your pardon?

GLUCK

Not Miss Gluck or Hannah Gluckstein, my abominable name, inflicted upon me by my Mother, simply Gluck, as in duck. No suffix, prefix or quotes. I believe titles are merely barriers, don't you?

CONSTANCE

Yes, yes, I suppose I do.

A beat as she looks at Gluck.

GLUCK

(Proffering a cigarette case from her trouser pocket) Cigarette?

CONSTANCE

Oh, no, thank you.

(A beat) I usually bring one of the girls to watch, but sometimes it is rather nice to work quite alone. You must find that yourself?

GLUCK

(Circling the pedestal) Yes indeed, there is a sweet elegance about working in a solitary fashion, that make one's art a form of communion, almost a form of prayer. Do you not agree?

CONSTANCE
Well, yes. Yes, I do.

GLUCK
And away from yourself?

CONSTANCE
I hadn't really thought about that...

GLUCK
You should. It is all part of the creative process. What we hide of ourselves, of our past and what we will allow into our work, to be seen. *(She steps back, admiring Constance's work.)* It's going to be magnificent, it really is, and so kind of Prudence to arrange all this.

CONSTANCE
Prudence has become a very good client, well friend, client and friend.

GLUCK
Can someone be both?

> *Constance smiles, not knowing what to say.*

Prue sent me these. *(She gestures towards an insignificant vase of pinks)* thanking me for god knows what! You know what she can be like! She'll send you a thank you note for a thank you note!

CONSTANCE
(Twinkling) Not from us, at least I don't remember the order.

GLUCK
(Looking at her, before:) Moyses Stevens I'm afraid.

CONSTANCE
(Laughing) I thought as much.

GLUCK
But from now on, I see I will be calling upon the expertise of the redoubtable Constance Spry.

CONSTANCE
You don't have to say that.

GLUCK
Because then I will be a client and not a friend?

CONSTANCE
(Slightly flustered) I didn't mean that.

GLUCK
I hope we can be both.

CONSTANCE
Well, then, you will be most welcome, I or one of my staff will—

GLUCK
Oh, I should insist on you to take all my commissions.

CONSTANCE
And I should be more than happy to.

GLUCK
Did you know it was Prue's husband who designed my studio?

CONSTANCE
No, no, I didn't.

GLUCK
You must come and see it. You know Prue trained to be an architect as well?

CONSTANCE
Hence her interest in interior design I suppose?

GLUCK
It seems a great pity to me that it is more accepted that she chooses drapes and cushions for society matrons while her husband actually creates something of lasting importance; there is still much work to do in that department.

CONSTANCE

But surely not for painters, artists like yourself? I admired your exhibition so much.

GLUCK

Thank you. I am fortunate that my work removes me from such trivialities as... cushions.

CONSTANCE

I wonder what that makes my humble arrangement? My flowers that will only have a life span of days.

GLUCK

(Going towards her and placing her hand on hers) It makes it the greatest of them all, the most fragile, but the most consequential for that very reason.

CONSTANCE

(Laughing brightly and placing her hand on Gluck's) That was the perfect answer.

GLUCK

And the truest.

> Pause. They unlock their grasp.

CONSTANCE

I met Prudence through my friend Syrie Maugham—do you know her?

GLUCK

We have not as yet met, though I have heard everyone talk about her. "White! White! White! No colour, it must all be white!" That is the mantra of Mrs. Maugham. (Laughing) Am I correct?

CONSTANCE

(Also laughing) I shouldn't laugh. She's very influential.

GLUCK

Really? Well I should like to meet her very much in that case. Can you arrange it? The wife of the novelist Somerset Maugham must be an interesting bird of paradise.

CONSTANCE

They are no longer married.

GLUCK

Caused quite a stink, didn't it? Well, if you can I should still like to meet her. And it is good to laugh at one's friends occasionally.

CONSTACE:

I would be happy to arrange a meeting.

GLUCK

Really? I should be most grateful. One always needs help with an artistic enterprise. *(A beat)* A marriage made in ambition I heard?

CONSTANCE

There are plenty of those in society. *(Looking at Gluck)* So often in life what you see isn't what you get!

GLUCK

You understand. *(She takes Constance's hand.)* That is refreshing. But do come and look at my studio. It's my sanctuary.

CONSTANCE

Won't I be interrupting your work?

GLUCK

But I interrupted it myself and such a pleasant form of interruption. *(Looking at the display)* They really are glorious. I've never seen flowers displayed in such a way before. No wonder all of London is abuzz with your name.

CONSTANCE

I believe that flower arranging is an art, though very different from painting. And I have very high standards, I won't allow any work that leaves the premises to be second rate. *(She breaks off, feeling she has said too much.)*

GLUCK

Please go on.

CONSTANCE

No, no, I'm sorry, I'm rattling on.

GLUCK

But I'm interested.

CONSTANCE

Well, though, as you say, I may be celebrated by society matrons, that 'art' can be achieved with the use of very little: a purse can be made from a pig's ear! Something beautiful should not just be an honour of the rich. Flowers for all occasions, for people from all walks of life. Call it the freemasonry of flowers! If I could, I would paint, but I cannot and so I paint using different materials. But the art of flower design has to change and be taken seriously: the sense of space, light, situation must all be taken into account. We can no longer merely cram common shop flowers such as carnations together and expect that to be enough; the world has changed. I want to see lime flowers, euphorbia and lilac, I want— *(She stops.)* Now I really have said too much!

GLUCK

Obviously you have a genius for flowers.

CONSTANCE

(Putting the few remaining flowers in the vase, a little embarrassed) Are you working towards another exhibition?

GLUCK

Yes, a portrait for it, but the subject is away and I'm reduced to painting in the drapes and hair. It's the sort of thing if I were famous I would give to one of my school to finish off!

CONSTANCE

But you are famous! Your work is becoming widely known, is it not?

GLUCK

Not enough for my liking. I am afraid I have ambition to be known as a great painter. It is just, well, with one thing and another, and the upkeep of this place— *(She breaks off, looks about her.)*

CONSTANCE
(Continuing with the arrangement) Well, I am sure you will be. There are some of us who think you are already.

GLUCK
And what does your husband, Mr. Spry, make of having a business woman for a wife?

CONSTANCE
Oh he is the business. Without Shav there wouldn't be Flower Decorations.

GLUCK
(Flatly) Really?

CONSTANCE
(Slightly uncomfortable) I don't recall there being an exhibition since 'Stage & Country'—such a clever name—in '26 wasn't it?.

GLUCK
Was it that long? Good heavens! Well, my mother has been keeping me busy of late, so I have had to put on hold one or two ideas that I had.

CONSTANCE
Mothers are often a burden aren't they?

GLUCK
I call my mother The Meteor. Does that answer your question?

CONSTANCE
(Knowingly) Perfectly. *(She puts in the last stem.)* Well, I think that is just about suitable.

GLUCK
(Standing back) Yes, yes, very fine. Very fine indeed.

CONSTANCE

Thank you. Would you like it to remain here, or would—

GLUCK

No, no, leave it there, then I can always see it. So beautiful. I am quite overwhelmed by it. Like a Dutch master—I am always so inspired by the Dutch masters.

Constance begins to pack up her equipment.

GLUCK *(cont.)*

I keep thinking, standing here, that I must paint them.

CONSTANCE

Really?

GLUCK

I haven't been so inspired by something for an age, what with The Meteor and all.

CONSTANCE

Meteor? Oh, yes.

GLUCK

It makes me want to cast all other work aside and begin at once.

CONSTANCE

I'm flattered, but how long will it take you to paint them? These blooms won't last forever in this heat.

GLUCK

Then you will have to return in a few days and do the design again! I insist upon it! Now will you please see my studio?

They smile at one another.

CONSTANCE

I should be delighted.

Gluck holds out her arm, like a man, and Constance puts hers through it and is led off.

GLUCK

I can't think how I'm going to pay for it!

CONSTANCE

(Looking about her. Smiling) Surely not?

GLUCK

(As they exit) You know, you're not at all as I imagined the famous Constance Spry to be.

> *Lights fade, music.*

> *Gluck continues to exit and Constance on walking off stage returns as before with her notes for a speech to the Women's Institute. She stands a moment on the semi lit stage, composing herself.*

FIVE

Lights up on the bare stage. **The Women's Institute, Chislehurst** *is projected, images of speakers giving talks. Constance appears, calm and happy as she addresses her captive audience. She still relies on notes to speak.*

CONSTANCE

Now, before I finish I must firstly thank you all for listening to this, one of my first little talks *(A reaction from the audience),* and secondly I want to say a few words about bulbs. *(Smiling, she produces a hyacinth bulb out of her pocket.)* It is never too early for this humble fellow, who can bring so much joy later in the year. By looking ahead and planting hyacinths, polyanthus, narcissi, Duc van Tol tulips and daffodils in pottery or china dishes, or even taking advantage of an old and unloved jelly mould, you and your home can enjoy colour and perfume for several months to come, certainly when the home needs it most. Don't forget to be aware of the size of container that you choose: as with everything, if you remember, never 'over vase' your materials! *(She smiles, a little breathless, surprised at how she has run on.)* Being so fond of the country, I prefer mine in natural groups and cover them in moss: this positively brings the woodland into the house! For me, this is preferable to odd single bulbs, usually hyacinths, dotted about the home higgledy piggledy, as we are unfortunately used to, and must break the habit of! *(She seems almost unaware as to her surroundings as she looks into the light.)* Don't let your prejudice about colour influence your choices either, or more importantly the choices of Nature and what she has made readily available to you. Just think how marvellous an array of orange crocuses and *Iris reticulata* could look together. Striking, but not impossible. 'Try anything once!' If you fail then at least be aware that you tried. *(Coming out of her 'reverie', she returns to her notes.)* Well, thank you, Ladies, Madam Chairwoman, for your time this afternoon. *(Remembering the bulb in her grasp)* And please do not forget our friend, the bulb. I cannot stress enough the pleasure that they can bring: just when you think winter has completely obliterated any hope of life, out they pop to remind you that hope isn't ever really lost upon us. A little like life!

> *Applause as lights fade. Music fades in. Constance smiles to her audience and enters the shop set, revealed from behind a curtain or screen. Placing the bulb back in her pocket, along with her notes, she takes a moment and removes her hat, checks her makeup in her compact before entering the next scene.*

SIX

*Images of London and of Constance Spry's shop, interior as well as exterior: **64, Audley Street, Flower Decorations Ltd.** is projected across the stage. As lights up, Rosemary, with an overall over her summer dress, is speaking on the telephone. Constance puts on her uniform/apron and is working on a large display of whitewashed and silver leaves; the container, a blackamoor, is positioned on a pedestal. She works around it muttering to herself, a pot of silver paint and brush beside her. There are other, identical, whitewashed displays on the floor or projected.*

ROSEMARY

Yes, yes, of course that will be fine. The earthenware jugs are cleaned and ready to be whitewashed, Syrie, and yes, I will tell her you telephoned as soon as she returns...Yes, yes, I will, thank you... Goodbye... yes, as soon as she returns. *(She bangs down the telephone.)* That woman!

CONSTANCE

Thank you, Rosemary. I just don't think I could cope with Syrie at this moment in time!

ROSEMARY

How are they coming along?

CONSTANCE

Slowly!

ROSEMARY

Well what Syrie wants, Syrie gets it would seem. So if you could call her when you get back from Lady Whoever I said, I'd greatly appreciate it!

CONSTANCE

Lady Portarlington.

ROSEMARY

Oh yes: eucalyptus, hydrangea and lichen branches.

CONSTANCE

The very same!

> *Val enters wearing a crisp, striped, buttoned dress and carrying a pad and pencil and a bunch of ivy and laburnum.*

VAL

(Overhearing) Madge Garland is going to be reporting on it.

ROSEMARY

On what?

VAL

On Lady P's ball of course!

CONSTANCE

(Diffusing the situation) However do you find these things out?

VAL

It's my job.

CONSTANCE

Syrie won't like that one jot!

VAL

Oh, was that her again! We've just had another like her on the shop telephone. The Prudence Maufe order that went to Hampstead, well, it's dying and needs replacing again. I thought it was a he at first, but I think not. Answers to the name of Gluck. I ask you!

Constance turns away and continues with her work.

VAL *(cont.)*

I did say that I imagined it would be nearly dead in this heat. I
doubt we could get the same flowers.

ROSEMARY

Well do you think you could go up to Ham—

VAL

Oh no, only wants Mrs. Spry to do it, as she has created 'such
magic'. I tried to explain that we had rather a lot on but—

ROSEMARY

And if you will let me interrupt you for a moment I am sure Mrs.
Spry will be able to manage it: if anyone can, she can!

Thank you, Val. And don't let that ivy rub up against you or—

VAL

(Interrupting her) Oh, it makes no difference. I seem immune to it.

(To Constance) Well, shall I say that you'll go tomorrow then?

CONSTANCE

There, done, I think that looks—

VAL

Suitable?

CONSTANCE

Well, we don't want to get stale do we? We must never get stale!

VAL

(Looking at the displays) And ten more to do? What a lot of trouble.
We should be charging the old bat more. I mean, look what you've
got in them. We should have just sent out white-washed kale leaves
and sold her that, for the amount she's paying!

42

CONSTANCE

Leave Syrie's account as it is please, Val.

VAL

Yes, Mrs. Spry, but you'll never make any money if you insist on not charging enough, especially for those that can afford it! I suppose Mrs. Maugham white-washes her account along with everything else.

ROSEMARY

Thank you, Val. I think I hear your telephone ringing.

VAL

(Listening) I can't hear anything.

ROSEMARY

It was a euphemism for that's enough, thank you.

VAL

Oh Lord, well I'll leave you to it then. *(Huffily)* You sure you don't want me to send someone through? I could send Nell!

CONSTANCE

No, no, it's quite alright. *(As she works, to herself)* She obviously hasn't finished the painting...

VAL

What?

Rosemary looks up at Constance, noticing a change in her.

CONSTANCE

Sorry? *(Quickly)* Oh, do try and encourage Nell, won't you? Make her see all the things that you see about the business, all the beauty and the positive things. Look for her potential.

VAL

I'm not a miracle worker.

ROSEMARY

Val! Really!

CONSTANCE

(Ignoring Val's remark) All the beauty of her surroundings.

VAL

I thought that's what you said in your last book about finding flowers in the hedgerows?

CONSTANCE

Well in that case, dear, think of her as a hedgerow.

We must cultivate all the girls, start them off and see what they can achieve. Those with skill we keep, and those without... we must inspire more effort.

Val merely looks at them both and exits.

ROSEMARY

(A beat) Oh that cheap scent! *(Wafting the air)* She distresses me, she really does.

CONSTANCE

Not as much as she distresses me!

ROSEMARY

You deserve a medal, you really do! *(A beat. She watches Constance adjust her design, and after a moment.)* Do you think these weekends in the country with Shav are really paying off?

CONSTANCE

To be frank, darling, Val is my ally in so many matters. She keeps things running like clockwork here, and she performs other duties that, well, that I'd rather not...

ROSEMARY

I shouldn't pry.

CONSTANCE

(Finishing a display. Smiling at Rosemary and taking her hand.) Right, on to the next! What a lark! Two down, eight to go!

ROSEMARY
So the Gluck order? *(A beat)* Connie, shall I speak to this Gluck and see if I can send someone else?

CONSTANCE
No. No, no... don't do that.

ROSEMARY
But won't you have your hands full with the Rothschild Ball?

> *Constance remains silent.*

ROSEMARY *(cont.)*
Well if you're sure, dear? Though, how many weeks has it been?

CONSTANCE
Quite sure, yes. There is always time in every day.

ROSEMARY
So who is this Gluck? It's a very strange name.

CONSTANCE
She's a painter, a wonderful painter and she has a studio in her home. Her work is quite extraordinary.

(Self-conscious. A beat) We should talk about the book.

> *Constance exits carrying the display. Rosemary attends to her paperwork. After a moment Constance returns with some more materials.*

ROSEMARY
Oh, whenever you like, I've plenty of ideas.

And she is painting your flower creation? That will be a first.

CONSTANCE
Now, I have plenty of ideas also. I'm very excited by the thought of a cookery book, and with your Cordon Bleu skills, well, how could we fail? *(A beat)* The business does need Val, you know, dear. She's a Martha, she's not a Mary. Who will get through life reliant on her wardrobe, she'll get by with her brain. We do need her.

ROSEMARY

Rubbish! The only person this business needs is you.

CONSTANCE

You're very loyal, Rosemary. But the business needs us all. I couldn't have painted all those leaves the other night for the shop windows, now, could I? And some of the girls didn't leave here till after midnight! And we and Val were here until two o'clock. Even if the finished result was worth it. No, Val has her area of expertise. I couldn't lose her.

ROSEMARY

I don't understand you. If I were in your shoes I should want to divorce Shav. *(Feeling she has said too much)* I'm sorry.

CONSTANCE

(Turning and staring at her) Divorce Shav?

ROSEMARY

Yes, dear. I've been thinking, thinking about it for weeks, I couldn't go on in your position. I realize that it will be very difficult for you, but if careful there should hardly be any scandal; it's not as if you're the Maughams! And—

CONSTANCE

(As if suddenly coming to her senses) Oh, but I couldn't do that! Don't be silly! I could never divorce Shav.

ROSEMARY

But why not?

CONSTANCE

(A beat) Because... Because, well, we are not married.

> Rosemary takes a step back, shocked, as blackout and music. Rosemary sets up the deckchairs as Constance, still lit, removes her shoes and apron.

SEVEN

Lights up, same as before, later. The shop has closed, no background sounds of the telephone etc. Constance and Rosemary sit in deckchairs, looking at the completed designs and sipping cups of tea.

CONSTANCE

Thank you for helping. Do you want some more tea? And there might be a bun left, I think there were some cream ones. *(She rises.)* I could check—

ROSEMARY

(Gesturing her to sit down) No, no, thank you, dear, please...

> *A beat*

CONSTANCE

I owe you an explanation, don't I?

ROSEMARY

Not at all, you don't—

CONSTANCE

No, I should like to tell you, to tell someone. Life can become very lonely, you know. Even when you are right in the heart of it.

ROSEMARY

Oh nonsense, you have friends, you have—

CONSTANCE

I have acquaintances, for whom I do the flowers.

ROSEMARY

The recurring problem of trade, as you see it?

Constance nods.

ROSEMARY *(cont.)*

But all that is changing, surely? Look at Syrie. A self made woman if ever there was one, and that is what you are, what we are in fact. And Spry girls go through the front door—these are career women.

CONSTANCE

I know dear, but I also know I have invested so much in this baby of mine, this business, that I have neglected other factors in my life, friendships being one of them. I know and accept that, but—

ROSEMARY

Something always has to give, of course it does—we're women.

CONSTANCE

(Smiles at Rosemary, then looks away) I was working in Ireland, working as a teacher. It was a long time ago. I thought I was in love —I shudder at the thought of it—a calf love, not a love to last, but then one never thinks of that at the time...

I soon realized that I had made a mistake, a very great mistake—the wedding night taught me that; what a ghastly affair the marriage bed is. A brutal business.

I'd wanted to get away from my mother, you see—

ROSEMARY

Well, we all feel like that at times.

CONSTANCE

No, this was different. She's a beastly woman. A meteor.

ROSEMARY

Meteor?

CONSTANCE

And because of her I found myself in a proper pickle and didn't know what to do about it.

ROSEMARY

And did he feel the same way?

CONSTANCE

James? James Marr, that was his name. I don't know how he felt.

ROSEMARY

(Hesitantly) I see.

CONSTANCE

(Almost matter-of-factly) Thankfully I have none of these problems to contend with now.

ROSEMARY

But where did you go? What did you do?

CONSTANCE

Well, my family were against my leaving James. Mother was vile, vile! She told me I had made my bed and so must lie in it. She adored James, you see. Just adored him, and he she. Sometimes I think she should have married him herself. Poor Father. But for me that marriage was a death sentence. A slow death sentence!

ROSEMARY

Oh, Connie.

> She places a hand on Constance's hand.

CONSTANCE

(After a moment, she rises and blows her nose) And then the Easter Rising happened. *(A beat)* I was working for the Red Cross by then, in their offices at Dublin Castle, and one moment everything was fine, and the next... I had heard the grumblings of the Irish, impossible not to, but all of a sudden a group of men, and women, had taken over buildings in the city, were pulling down the British flag. They had guns, pistols, rifles! *(To Rosemary suddenly)* Well,

I'd never known anything like it. I was immediately called upon: makeshift beds, bandages made out of God knows what, begging for food and coal. How we managed! How I improvised! We were shot at, Rosemary! The Red Cross shot at! And yet it all seemed to come out of nothing, a peaceful Easter day. A beautiful sunny day.

Of course many were furious, furious! So angry that their holiday had been interrupted...

ROSEMARY

I can imagine.

CONSTANCE

...but then the Irish were punished, and that soon changed people's minds. So many shot. They didn't need to do that. They didn't seem to care. One of the ringleaders was so badly injured that he had to be strapped to a chair before he could be executed.

But they still shot him.

> *Rosemary rises and goes to Constance.*

I'm alright, really I am. It's so strange to speak of it, that's all.

(Smiling, blowing her nose again) So, you see, after all that I just knew I couldn't stay, knew I had to do something with my life. It was such a jolt to the senses. *(A beat. More her normal self)* And I wasn't getting any younger. So I came back to England, and then I met Shav.

ROSEMARY

So you're really Mrs. Marr? But why didn't you divorce this husband of yours?

CONSTANCE

Oh I did, I did. It was all above board, believe me. I'm not Mrs. Marr at all. I'm... Mrs. Nothing.

ROSEMARY

Well, I don't understand then.

CONSTANCE

Shav was married too. He still is.

ROSEMARY

Oh, Connie! What if this got out? It could be the end of Flower Decorations. Could be the end of us all!

Constance rises and begins to collect up the arrangements.

CONSTANCE

(Turning her back to her, as if like a naughty child) Please don't be cross with me, darling. I don't think I could cope with that tonight.

Rosemary rises and turns Constance towards her.

ROSEMARY

How could I be cross with someone who has done so much for me?CONSTANCE

Shav's wife won't give him a divorce, absolutely refuses to, so... Time went on and...Well, time went on. It stopped being important and as the business grew I didn't really have time to even think about it. It didn't seem important anymore. You do see? I want you to see. I want someone to see. To know.

(Brighter) If I don't think about it, it isn't happening! There is always so much to do and— *(Catching sight of the clock)* My, look at the time! We should be home and in bed. You go, dear, I can lock up.

ROSEMARY

Certainly not! We'll go together.

Constance embraces Rosemary. Then, for a moment, they clear the displays off stage, quickly and silently.

ROSEMARY *(cont.)*

You never speak of your mother. Is she still alive?

CONSTANCE

As far as I know.

ROSEMARY

You mean you don't know?

CONSTANCE

If I receive a card at Christmas I know she is—

ROSEMARY
Connie!

CONSTANCE
James looks after her. *(She packs the penultimate display away. Rosemary picks up the last.)* There all done, now up the wooden hill to Bedfo—

ROSEMARY
What do you mean James looks after her? Your husband, looks after your mother?

CONSTANCE
Ex husband. *(Firmly)* Shav is my husband.

ROSEMARY
(Standing still, the display still in her hand) You never mentioned any of this before.

CONSTANCE
There was no reason to. I never think of it.

> *Music. As the lights fade Rosemary remains standing, looking at her as Constance dons a new apron and puts on her shoes again. Rosemary then packs up the deckchairs and draws the curtain upon the shop area of the stage before exiting.*

EIGHT

Images of Hampstead, as before. Projection, as before: **The Studio, Bolton House**. *Late Summer. Constance once again at the pedestal working on the same group of flowers, and Gluck, wearing painting smock, over male attire, at her easel, painting the white arrangement. Constance's overall this time is more summerlike as lights up. The couple are in mid conversation, very easy with each other. A bucket of extra white flowers is at Constance's side. She places the last few stems into the arrangement. A gramophone plays softly.*

GLUCK

(Commenting on the bucket) So many extra flowers this week.

CONSTANCE

(Brightly) No, no these are... well for something else. *(Slightly embarrassed, not looking at Gluck)* I had thought that I might make a new arrangement for you, from me. To thank you for so many pleasant mornings. *(Quickly)* But still white. All white.

GLUCK

That is Mrs. Maugham's influence upon you.

CONSTANCE

A white room, Syrie says, is a blank canvas.

I'm forever battling the endless clutter of rooms, my flowers fighting for breath amongst the stifling surroundings they find themselves in. Syrie strips all such conformity away. Everything in a Syrie Maugham interior is as a painter would have arranged his, or her, subject. *(Plunging her hands into the bucket of water and pulling up some of the flowers)* There is such comfort in a bucket of flowers and the endless possibilities of them. Just water, a bucket and flowers.

GLUCK

(Laughing) Yes, yes, I see that.

CONSTANCE

I've been preaching! I apologize. When I am here I always seem to preach!

GLUCK

Not at all. I have never known you to preach, ever, during all our many conversations.

CONSTANCE

I'm so looking forward to your meeting Syrie.

GLUCK

And I.

CONSTANCE

(Quietly) To tell you the truth I shall rather miss our mornings of conversation.

GLUCK

And you thought that you might continue the exercise with another arrangement?

CONSTANCE

(An intake of breath) No, just a way of thanking you. *(They smile.)* And you haven't changed your mind about the title? It is still to be called 'Alba'?

GLUCK

Connie, I shall miss these mornings very much also.

> Gluck comes towards her and takes the flowers from her and replaces them in the bucket.

GLUCK *(cont.)*

Your hands are wet. Here, let me.

> *She removes her smock and proceeds to dry Constance's hands in it. The process is done in silence. After a moment Constance looks up.*

CONSTANCE

Your smock.

> *Gluck remains holding her hands in hers.*

GLUCK

What does it matter?

> *Gluck takes her hands and kisses them.*

CONSTANCE

Gnarled old hands! An old woman's hands.

GLUCK

Please don't make light of it, Connie. I want to.

CONSTANCE

(Breathlessly) I...

GLUCK

Please say I don't need to explain.

I mean, look at me! *(Moving away, lighting a cigarette)* My mother refers to it as a, as a kink in the brain. She hasn't tried to understand, finds it repellent, despicable, and to a degree hates me for it. I painted her some time ago, and it's there on the canvas. I didn't paint it, but her disgust of me comes through in every brush stroke. You might not see it, but it follows me around the room, to such a degree that I can't actually look at it. I avoid her gaze on canvas and in life. *(She stubs out her cigarette.)*

CONSTANCE

I don't know what to say. I...

GLUCK

(Taking her hands again) Say that you are my friend. Say that you

understand. Say that even when this picture is finished we will be as we are now.

CONSTANCE

(Almost shaking. Trying to make light of the situation) If it isn't finished soon you'll be adding holly and mistletoe!

GLUCK

(Angrily) Don't make light of it. Why must you always make light of things, things that matter?

CONSTANCE

Sorry. *(A beat)* I make light of things because I hate so the thought of being dull, of boring I suppose.

I make light because...

GLUCK

Because it is easier than facing the truth?

CONSTANCE

I don't have this new vogue for looking in and then letting it all out. You're lucky.

GLUCK

Lucky!

CONSTANCE

Yes! I'm a child of Victoria. I want to, believe me, I want to, but...

GLUCK

Yes?

CONSTANCE

Give me time. This is alien to me, this is... *(A beat)* I have a marriage, Gluck. I can't have anything jeopardizing that, and most importantly, I have a business, a business I have waited so long for.

GLUCK

(Putting her arms about Constance's shoulders) I understand.

CONSTANCE
You do?

GLUCK
Your passion is your work. And not your husband's.

CONSTANCE
Did you say husband? Or husband's?

GLUCK
That is for you to interpret.

A beat.

CONSTANCE
(Returning to her work) I read recently that 'A woman is either happily married or an interior decorator'.

GLUCK
But what if it didn't have to be like that. What if there was an all-fulfilling passion that overtook one?

CONSTANCE
But I have that already: my work.

GLUCK
May I challenge that work for your affection, Connie?

She goes to Constance and takes her face in her hands. Constance doesn't resist.

And you don't find this—I mean you don't find me despicable?

CONSTANCE
No... No, I don't.

Constance rests her head on Gluck's shoulder, and Gluck kisses her hair as the light fades. Music. Gluck exits and Constance takes a chair that will be on the stage/rostrum of the next set and tries to compose herself, overcome by what has happened. The dim light flickers above her, signifying a passing of time. She rises again, walks up and down. Takes off a shoe and squeezes a toe. Puts on the shoe and walks up and down again trying to calm herself. Pressing her handkerchief to her brow. After a moment she dons a new jacket and hat.

NINE

Swanley College is projected across the stage. Images of college and floristry students. Lights up on a bare stage except for a college chair and a pedestal upon which sits a white urn containing ivy, snowberry, Love Lies Bleeding and branches. Constance, dressed as before—though she has added a scarf—inserts white Christmas roses to the almost complete arrangement. She is giving a floristry class to a group of students. Although not seen, her audience is responsive vocally. Note she has abandoned any use of notes. She finishes.

CONSTANCE

Oh, thank you. It has been such a pleasure, this afternoon, a real tonic for me. Thank you, Dr. Barrett, for inviting me to Swanley College. The last time I gave a speech to a group of girls was when I was working for the Red Cross and giving instruction to some trainee nurses, on how to bandage an injured soldier! I do hope you will have me back at some point. *(A beat)* Next month? Thank you. And at least there will be a little more to look forward to in the garden, and therefore in the vase! And please note, girls, it need not be the variegated ivy—any will do just as well. Naturally, the roses need not be white, but I do think they have a splendour that cannot be equalled at this time of the year, and certainly they should not be mixed with other colours: with white flowers their own delicate beauty is best seen alone.

Always remember to trust your first instinct, and never forget to develop your own style: then and only then will you ripen as an artist.

(A beat, she collects herself) Now then, any questions? After which I think Dr. Barrett has promised us a splendid tea!

> *The sound of the students fades into music as the scene fades out. Constance exits.*

TEN

Syrie Maugham's residence, Chelsea is projected across the stage. Images of London and Syrie Maugham interiors: all white. Party music, jazz, as lights up on an indication of Syrie's famous all white sitting room. Mirror and glass sparkle, a Spry flower display. The sounds of a party underway. Syrie enters, followed by Shav, Val and Rosemary, all dressed for a party. Syrie, 6os, is over-bearing, monstrous and acid. She, like Constance, is a survivor. She has a winning charm when she wants something. She is dressed, fussily and dowager-like and to complement her She sometimes mispronounces words. Shav is in evening dress, Rosemary in black and Val in a patterned silk (the design is one of lupins) which doesn't quite suit her. Val and Shav smoke, as does Syrie, though more for effect.

SYRIE

(Ushering her guests in, mid conversation. Sounds of the party off) And here we are! Something of a departure I think you'd agree? My all-white drawing room. All white! Careful of the rug tassels.

They all look around with varying degrees of appreciation.

ROSEMARY

(Respectful and businesslike, knowing that however difficult Syrie is, she is still a client) No wonder it has taken the world by storm.

SYRIE

I knew you would understand, my dear. I knew someone who worked so closely with Connie would understand.

SHAV

All of London is talking about it, I hear.

SYRIE

Well, of course they are!

ROSEMARY

And don't the flowers work well? Connie was right of course.

VAL

Of course, she always is.

SYRIE

They've held up haven't they? Considering I've been moving them from surface to surface. Bang, bang bang! Until, lo and behold, they're back where I originally put them!

VAL

I thought Connie chose that focus point?

SYRIE

One should always trust one's instincts.

SHAV

Really? You think?

SYRIE

Well certainly in design. No?

ROSEMARY

Well I think you've proved yourself right.

SYRIE

Connie understands my theory so well.

SHAV

Oh?

SYRIE

That in design, elimination is the secret to its success.

SHAV

And in life also?

SYRIE

(She chuckles) You mean husbands?

VAL

(Before she can stop herself) You've been married before?

SYRIE

(Looking at Val, summing her up before answering) Of course I have. I was married to Henry Wellcome, of Burroughs Wellcome, the pharmaceutical company, before he divorced me.

VAL

(Embarrassed) Oh.

SYRIE

No need to be embarrassed. I had the last laugh; I had doormats made, for all my homes, with WELCOME embossed on them. I adored watching my guests wipe their feet!

> *Shav roars with laughter. Syrie looks at him knowingly.*

ROSEMARY

(Quickly changing the subject) I can't think what could have become of them. Can you, Shav?

SYRIE

I can't abide lateness.

SHAV

(Still laughing) But Syrie, you're notoriously late!

SYRIE

And that is why I can't abide it in others!

> *Shav and Val move away a little. They study the walls.*

VAL

(To Shav) It looks like a dowager's idea of an operating theatre.

SHAV

(Guides Val away) It isn't like Connie to be—

SYRIE

I can't either. Can you, Rosemary? Can you, Val? It is Val isn't it?

VAL

Yes, it's short for Valmer.

SYRIE

How unusual. As you say, Shav dear, totally out of character! Oh, I'm so pleased you're looking around.

SHAV

What is?

SYRIE

Why Connie's non-appearance. Her lateness at my launch. What else could I have meant?

SHAV

(Somewhat uncomfortable) Maybe she popped into the shop on her way back from Hampstead.

ROSEMARY

That must be it!

SYRIE

Hampstead? Oh, yes, Hampstead. It's a part of the world I don't know terribly well. Quite a separate race I understand. Run by the women I hear. The Amazons.

They all laugh politely.

VAL

But what could she want from the shop?

SYRIE

A woman and her work are never parted, Valmer.

VAL

Val.

SYRIE

That is what I said. And this Miss Gluck derives from Hampstead. does she not?

SHAV

Just Gluck.

ROSEMARY

Yes, that's correct.

SYRIE

Yes and yes? Only Gluck and Hampstead?

ROSEMARY

Yes. Yes and yes.

SYRIE

How peculiar. Well, if Connie wants me to meet this Gluck then of course I will. I know she won't be wasting my time. From what she has said she seems to have a positive passion for her!

ROSEMARY

The mirrors are—

SYRIE

A revelation! Aren't they just.

ROSEMARY

I've never been particularly fond of mirror myself but—

SYRIE

I don't hold with any of that piffle. Make the best with what you have, for there is always someone uglier than you are.

ROSEMARY

(Embarrassed) Yes, thank you, Syrie, I will.

SYRIE

I bet Connie isn't forever looking at herself in the mirror. Isn't that right, Shav?

SHAV

(Looking about) No, no, certainly not. Doesn't even possess one of these blasted compacts women are always looking in these days.

SYRIE

Well someone like Connie doesn't need one, does she? No time!

(Playfully) Not paying you enough attention I suppose!

SHAV

Oh, I wouldn't say that.

> *Val catches his eye.*

SYRIE

She's like me. She is one of society's new breed, new woman. She believes she can have it all: a husband and a career, or a career and a home life.

VAL

And is that possible? Can a woman achieve contentment in the workplace as well as her home life?

SYRIE

(Looking at her again, as if for the first time) Are you one of the new breed then?

VAL

Well, I just wondered if it was possible, that was all.

SYRIE

To my mind nobody is remembered for having a happy marriage.

> *The drifting back and forth of the group continues as Rosemary now breaks off.*

SYRIE *(cont.)*

Do look around, dear. Feel free to trespass! Everyone else has been in now. I like to bring people in in groups. It's easier for them to get the effect I've been looking for, if they're not forever nattering to each other! So do, do look.

ROSEMARY

Thank you.

SYRIE

And then I like to hear what people think when they depart. It's a little like Somerset ear-wigging after one of his plays as the audience leaves the theatre!

SHAV

Not that it will make a blind bit of difference!

SYRIE

And what do you mean by that?

SHAV

Well, if I know you, you will still hold to your original instincts.

SYRIE

Naughty! You're mixing things up there, Shav. This is my house: it was part of the settlement, it can never be taken away from me. So I may do as I like in it.

SHAV

Point taken. And what of Somerset these days—any news?

SYRIE

Why should I have any news? Too much time amongst women has sharpened your claws, Shav. I suggest some male company.

SHAV

Like Somerset!

Val giggles.

SYRIE

(With a token of warmth) Despicable man! *(To Rosemary)* But what I was going to say to you, Rosemary dear, was, well for instance, look what Cecil has done to his bathroom. Drawn around the hands of all his friends, on the wall! I ask you! And got them to sign their own palms! Not to everyone's taste, but, in fact it has caused something of a stir and the orders have been pouring in for him. *(To Shav)* So, like Mr. Beaton, what I do with the decor of my home is my business—

SHAV

Then why do you listen at doorways?

SYRIE

Because I'm a business woman. Haven't you met one before?

ROSEMARY

Touché, Syrie.

SYRIE

Rosemary understands, Shav. She happens to be a business woman herself.

SHAV

So open house paves the way to your shop front?

SYRIE

(With weight) I am my shop front.

ROSEMARY

(To Val) You're very quiet. What do you think?

SYRIE

She's soaking it all up, no doubt! Learning.

VAL

I was just wondering how your clients are supposed to keep it clean.

SYRIE

(Acidly) Well, I would have thought that rather depended upon

their domestic arrangements.

Now if you have all seen enough, shall we return to the others?

> *The doors open and Constance and Gluck enter. Gluck, smoking, dressed in full male evening attire and Constance in an evening gown, looking very fetching.*

CONSTANCE

They said you were in here. Syrie, darling, I can't tell you how sorry we are!

GLUCK

Indeed, many apologies, Mrs. Maugham, and thank you for inviting me to your charming home.

CONSTANCE

(Looking about her) Oh my. My goodness! What a transformation!

VAL

(To Shav) And not just the room. Watch her now, she has already seen it, she put the flowers in, but she will pretend she's—

SHAV

Shut up, Val! *(Going to Constance, leaving Val decidedly miffed. He kisses Constance lightly.)* We were going to send out a search party!

CONSTANCE

Well, really, Syrie, I can hardly believe it. I think it's wonderful, don't you, Gluck?

GLUCK

Indeed I do, Connie.

CONSTANCE

What was that, Shav?

SHAV

It doesn't matter. *(He goes towards Gluck and shakes her hand.)* How do you do, Gluck?

GLUCK

(Stubbing out her cigarette) Ah, of course. Very well, thank you.

CONSTANCE

(Introducing people to Gluck) And this is Rosemary, my Man Friday! And Val, the real labourer in the garden, and of course Mrs. Maugham.

Gluck, Rosemary and Val shake hands and exchange hellos. Rosemary and Val break off and admire a painting.

SYRIE

And the flowers are a triumph! The arums— *(Pronounced incorrectly)*

CONSTANCE

Arums, darling.

SYRIE

Indeed. The antirrhinums— *(Also pronounced incorrectly)*

CONSTANCE

(Jolly) Antirrhinums, Syrie.

VAL

Snapdragons.

SYRIE

Precisely! *(To Constance)* I was so right to have them there.

CONSTANCE

(Twinkling) Of course you were, Syrie. I'm so pleased you're happy. *(Looking around again)* Well, I really think this is your best yet: so innovative of you. Beautifully overscaled.

SYRIE

If only those ghastly arts and crafts people understood that!

ROSEMARY

(To Gluck) And Mrs. Spry was so particular to get it right. She did the design again and again... Well, she always does get it right, however long it takes.

CONSTANCE

Your best. Don't you think, Shav?

SHAV

Syrie has the knack of staying one step ahead of the trend.

SYRIE

Well, it's a little more than that, I hope!

CONSTANCE

Of course it is. What a thing to say, Shav.

GLUCK

I agree. I think the triumph of this space, and I agree with Connie that it is a triumph, is the marrying of so many different styles and creating a harmony within them. Set off by the fact that this is not a blank canvas—the main player in this room is in fact *the canvas.*

> *There is a brief pause, as all the guests look at each other, then at their surroundings.*

SYRIE

(Going towards Gluck and taking her hand) That, of course, was my intention. How perceptive of you—may I call you Gluck?—how discerning of you to gauge immediately what I had in mind.

SHAV

(Looking into his empty glass) All way above my head I am afraid. Would you mind if I refreshed my drink?

SYRIE

(Her hand still over Gluck's) What? Oh, help yourself, Shav, and anyone else who wants one. I don't know where those damn waiters are. *(Looking at Val)* Next time I think I'll employ florists!

> *The group, with the exception of Val, laughs.*

SHAV

Well, if you'll excuse me, ladies and— *(He stops himself.)* Well, if you will excuse me, can I get anyone a top up?

VAL

Yes, I should like another.

SYRIE

Run along then, my dear. You can go now.

(As Val and Shav exit) Such an original dress.

ROSEMARY

(Following through the open door, whispers to Constance) Lupins! I'll get you both something to drink.

     Constance roars with laughter. Syrie and Gluck look at her.

GLUCK

Darling?

SYRIE

(Noting the use of "Darling") Yes indeed! Darling Connie, what is it? What's so funny?

CONSTANCE

Oh, I'm sorry, it's just a little tease Rosemary and I share.

SYRIE

Well, I think you should share it with us!

CONSTANCE

Lupins can be poisonous!

SYRIE

Well, I'm still in the dark. Doesn't the word derive from wolf?

GLUCK

No, that is lupine.

SYRIE

How clever of you.

CONSTANCE

Well anyway, it's all practically the same thing.

SYRIE

My dear, I'm not sure you should have a cocktail after all.

The night air has intoxicated you! *(Her manner changing)* Now then! Down to business.

CONSTANCE

(Still laughing) Whatever do you mean?

SYRIE

There is a reason why we do everything. And the reason, the reason Gluck is here tonight is to see what we can do to help her.

GLUCK

You're very direct.

SYRIE

At my age, a woman has no other choice! One might be dead before one gets to the end of the sentence!

CONSTANCE

Thank you, Syrie. I knew you would help.

SYRIE

Well, I shall make sure I get something out of it as well. I always do—but I don't see why an exhibition at the Fine Arts Society wouldn't be in order.

GLUCK

You could arrange that?

SYRIE

You'd have to do the running yourself—I'm not a skivvy—but I could put you in touch with the necessary people.

CONSTANCE

Oh, Gluck, isn't that kind!

SYRIE

I take it you have the means to finance such a venture.

CONSTANCE

Well, of course she has, and Gluck has a marvellous idea of how to frame her work, quite simple, but so effective.

SYRIE

(She runs her fingers along Constance's arm. Perceptively) I see you have a champion in Connie.

GLUCK

I'm very fortunate.

SYRIE

Indeed. I'll make some calls in the morning.

I think an all-white background for your exhibition. No?

GLUCK

Yes, of course.

SYRIE

And these frames you talk of, tell me about them. Also white?

GLUCK

Most definitely.

CONSTANCE

Gluck finds traditional gilt frames cumbersome for her delicate, free style.

SYRIE

As do I. So draining, so yesterday.

CONSTANCE

(Excited) Gluck's frames are none of those things. They are simply three tiers of wood, surrounding the painting, but fitted to the wall and painted the same colour.

SYRIE

The same colour!

CONSTANCE

Or paper. The effect is startling, suddenly the emphasis is completely upon the painting and everything else merges into—

SYRIE

(Transfixed at the thought of them) So everything else is eliminated?

GLUCK

Precisely.

CONSTANCE

Oh, I knew you would understand. Not everyone is keen on them—

SYRIE

Then they are idiots.

GLUCK

Thank you, Mrs. Maugham.

SYRIE

Syrie, please. And have you had them patented yet?

GLUCK

I'm looking into it.

SYRIE

I wouldn't. All that can be rather a nasty minefield. No need to amongst friends.

GLUCK

You think?

SYRIE

(Changing the subject) And you've brought some canvases to show me? *(To Constance)* Of course, I trust your judgment implicitly, my dear.

CONSTANCE

One in particular I'm especially fond of: it's called 'Alba'. It's of the first floral display I ever created for Gluck. All white!

SYRIE

Really! We have much in common it seems.

GLUCK

(Gesturing towards the door) Shall we?

SYRIE

(Looking at her intently) I can't wait, I feel at the beginning of something beautiful!

And I must introduce you to my dear friend Nesta Obermer. I think she'll be thrilled by you and your exhibition, Gluck, thrilled!

> *Gluck takes Syrie's arm and guides her out of the drawing room, followed by Connie, who takes one last look at the white interior and smiles, radiantly happy.*
>
> *The lights fade. Sounds of the party in the rest of the house. Music.*

ELEVEN

The Fine Arts Society, London *is projected across the stage. Images of gallery exhibitions follow. The music gives way to the sound of carpenters, workmen, banging, preparation. Lights up slowly on an all white stage. A workman, in overalls and cap, his back to the audience, is putting the last piece of the distinctive styled 'Gluck' frame together. The frame is designed so that although bearing the characteristics of a frame, it is attached to the wall, like a molding, and painted the same colour as the wall. This blends with its background, therefore not detracting from the painting itself. As the workman departs, the room becomes bathed in white light and the painting 'Alba' is projected into the frame. The sounds of workmen etc. fades into the noise of an appreciative audience at an exhibition. The noise intensifies.*

Blackout.

Interval.

TWELVE

*Winter 1935. Images of the East End of London, then schools in the area, school children, slums etc. **Stepney School** is projected onto the stage. An audience of working-class school children is implied as lights up on a serviceable table. Constance enters and stands behind it. She wears a smart day suit, hat and her ropes of pearls. She is less radiant than when she last gave a talk. She makes a big effort to be engaging. On the table are cabbage leaves, shells, a few autumn flowers, some leaves and grasses. She holds some flowers as she gives her talk. Sounds of the children.*

CONSTANCE

Good morning, children, and thank you for inviting me back. And I must let you into a little secret—something I didn't tell you last time—that it wasn't so very long ago I was a headmistress at a school very like yours, in fact quite near here, in Homerton.

(Looking at her audience) Now! I know Mrs. Hughes asked you to bring in things from home that we could use in a flower arrangement, and I've been very impressed by your choices. I want this to be a flower arrangement that doesn't have to use flowers, that doesn't have to cost very much, or in fact cost anything! I wanted you to see that many others things, things that we take for granted and don't really look at, can take on a sort of beauty, that we can use instead of flowers.

Now somebody asked me when I came in which is my least favourite flower; well, I will tell you: the chrysanthemum. Horrible, horrible! I won't have them in any of my displays, not for all the tea in China!

(Holding up some large leaves) I would rather have these sturdy cabbage leaves, arranged decoratively, gracing my table. *(She looks into her audience.)* So thank you for bringing in the cabbage leaves, Percy.

Now look at these, children. *(Holding up some grasses)* Now these can be picked anywhere. You might actually be doing someone a good deed by picking their overgrown grass for them! *(While she has been talking she has been arranging the grasses in a jar.)* And see how fetching that looks in an old pickling jar—very serviceable. Perhaps some of the boys could try that? *(She looks around the room and chuckles.)* And it doesn't have to be grasses: what about willowherb, with its leaves stripped, or wild parsnip, oats or wheat? *(She holds up a simple seashell.)* Now who brought this in? Had someone been to the seaside and brought you back one? It's a lovely shell, and just right for a late flowering rose that you might see somewhere.

You see, sometimes we find things that make us happy, that are exciting to the eye, beautiful to look at, in the most unexpected of places! And for a few pence, or for nothing at all, you really can be a millionaire.

> *The lights dim to black. Music.*
>
> *Constance steps away from the table and exits.*

THIRTEEN

The Spry Residence, London is projected across the stage. The hallway of the Sprys' London home again. As lights up Shav is visible though the open door to his study. He is on the telephone. He is dressed in evening attire, though he still has to add his bow tie and cufflinks.

SHAV

We'll discuss it tonight, I promise... no, she'll be in Hampstead... I'm not turning a blind eye to anything... I shall be late if I don't get a move on and you know how that irritates you... I'll talk to her about it!... She can't be missing that much time from the shop, she wouldn't... Just not at the moment, I don't know which way the wind is blowing... I don't know what is going on... yes, yes I'm sure you do... Please, darling, don't be like that... I must go, I'll pick you up at seven, I hear her... Of course I do. *(The caller hangs up.)* Bloody bitch. *(He replaces the receiver and sighs.)*

Constance enters from the staircase carrying a small, overnight suitcase and a coat on her arm. She is in an evening dress and cloak. Shav enters the hall quietly.

CONSTANCE

Lord, you startled me!

SHAV

Sorry, Connie. *(Noticing the suitcase)* I didn't think you were staying in Hampstead again.

CONSTANCE

(Putting the suitcase down) It just seemed to make sense. Gluck has some guests, and she wants to talk about the possibility of another exhibition. I'm going to speak to Syrie about it.

SHAV

Well you won't get a penny out of that dried up fossil! You didn't the last time. Don't know how Gluck got the damn thing on.

CONSTANCE

As a matter of fact Syrie has been very encouraging about the idea.

SHAV

Just don't invite me along.

CONSTANCE

I know how you feel about them both.

SHAV

(Going to her) I don't mean to, it's just one I find irritating and the other... anxious-making. For one so calm, Connie, you do seem to attract the strangest associates.

CONSTANCE

Calm? Neither can help it. One has been neglected by her mother, when she needed her—well, we all know about that—and the other by her husband.

SHAV

Somerset Maugham neglecting his wife! She should have banked on that when she forced the poor old brute to marry her!

CONSTANCE

So your sympathy is with him?

SHAV

It most certainly is! She's enough to change anyone!

CONSTANCE

I see... Well, whether she did or did not, doesn't detract from the fact that she, like Gluck, is my customer. I can't not take an interest if I want the business to prosper. *Our* business Shav.

SHAV

But you do like them.

CONSTANCE

Yes, I do. They both have qualities... I really should be on my way.

SHAV

Did you see the piece in the *Standard*? Cabbage leaves are king!

CONSTANCE

(Smiling) And how nice *Vogue* was. And next year I know what we'll do—

SHAV

(Eagerly) Yes?

CONSTANCE

I thought we could introduce— *(She catches site of the clock, picking up her suitcase again, coming to her senses.)* Lord, look at the time!

SHAV

(Disappointed) Do you not find her anxious-making?

CONSTANCE

Who?

SHAV

Gluck, of course. Do you not find her somewhat queer, apart from her appearance and general demeanour?

CONSTANCE

(Irritated) I rather like the way she dresses. I think it rather brave. So unfussy. I wish I could express myself the way she does.

SHAV

I'll have to lock my dressing room!

CONSTANCE

Don't be tiresome. *(Putting suitcase down again. Passionately)* She manages to communicate to the world, not only on canvas, but also by the clothes she wears. Elsa Schiaparelli is designing something for her at the moment. I believe it will turn heads.

SHAV

And you don't think dressing like a man already does?

CONSTANCE

Who is being a cat now?

SHAV

The circles you now... circulate in, Constance.

CONSTANCE

(Growing angry) We, Shav, we circulate in.

SHAV

Elsa Schiaparelli, Syrie Maugham... Ireland must seem—

CONSTANCE

Don't mention Ireland, Shav! I've asked you that before. Now will you just— *(She holds up her hands in frustration.)* Will you just let things...be. For God's sake! I won't have you snip, snip, snipping away at Gluck, I won't! *(Turning on him savagely)* Or I could say something! I really could.

SHAV

(Taken aback. Quietly) I'm sorry.

CONSTANCE

Yes, others would be sorry too.

　　He tries to take her hand.

Don't! *(A beat. Composing herself. She sighs. Slightly shocked by herself)* No, I'm sorry.

SHAV

So am I.

CONSTANCE

We aren't going to make waves for each other are we, Shav?

SHAV

No, no. I don't want that. *(A beat)* Would you? *(He fishes his cufflinks out of his pocket and holds out his wrists. He smiles at her.)*

CONSTANCE

(A beat. She smiles, also.) It's part of a wife's duties, isn't it? And I'm still the same Connie as I was then. It's just I'm doing something that makes me...

SHAV

Go on.

CONSTANCE

(As she attaches the cufflinks) Well, well, makes me feel I'm alive I suppose. It's so difficult to put into words... Besides we both wanted the same things. Didn't we? Haven't we? We still both want the same things, enjoy the same things: our love of flowers, gardening, design! We still have that don't we?

SHAV

(She has finished. He withdraws his wrists.) Yes, yes we do. But are you talking about business or something else?

CONSTANCE

We have so much, Shav. Just the conversations over dinner are... well, give me such happiness. And I've long ago given up the belief that a marriage is the bringing together of two halves and making a whole like a cross pollination of tulips! That is not what this, this marriage is. I see that now. Let's not spoil anything, please.

SHAV

We have changed. This business has changed us. As well as—

CONSTANCE

(Touching him) Nothing has really changed for me, even after all this time. You're still the golden thread that runs through my life.

SHAV

(Looking at her) I like it when you're still. You so often aren't.

CONSTANCE

(Brighter) Because there is so much to do! There is always the next big thing!

SHAV

I do love you, Connie.

CONSTANCE

Where did that come from?

SHAV

And at least you're still dressing like a female!

> Constance laughs and plants a kiss on his cheek affectionately.

When will you be back?

CONSTANCE

Tomorrow, of course.

SHAV

And will you be at the shop tomorrow?

CONSTANCE

Yes. Why wouldn't I be?

SHAV

I just wondered.

CONSTANCE

And if I wasn't at the shop tomorrow Rosemary would be more than capable of managing things in my absence...

SHAV

Of course.

CONSTANCE

...with Val's assistance. *(She collects up the suitcase and holds it shield-like towards her body, protectively.)* Now, I need to be on my way. Good night, Shav.

> *She goes to the door, but then turns back.*

And where are you off to this evening? So Dapper Dan.

You wouldn't have been able to come to Hampstead even if I had wanted you to. Would you?

SHAV

I have a dinner that I need to attend.

CONSTANCE

(Knowingly) Ah. Goodnight then, Shav. I'll see you tomorrow.

SHAV

Goodnight, Constance. *(Exiting into the study)*

> *Constance opens her handbag, gets out her compact, checks her appearance, before opening the door and exiting into the street.*

> *The lights fade. Music.*

> *Constance walks to a lit area at the front of the stage and removes her cloak, revealing a nightgown. She discards this and her evening slippers and enters the scene.*

FOURTEEN

Images of Gluck's successful exhibition at the Fine Arts Society. These fade into 1930s postcards of Cornwall. **Penreath Cottage, Cornwall** *is projected across the stage. Gluck in men's pajamas smokes a cigarette at the open door. It is night, a gramophone plays Billie Holiday singing: 'Your Mother's Son-in-Law'. Gluck tosses the cigarette butt into the night and turns to Constance, asleep on large kilim cushions, on the floor. She is dressed in a linen nightgown, a gypsy style shawl/or the cloak draped over her. The light of the hearth still lingers. The record stops. Gluck goes to turn the record over.*

CONSTANCE

(Stirring) No, don't.

GLUCK

No? Very well, whatever you wish.

CONSTANCE

Let's just enjoy the evening. No, night—what do I mean? I really should be in bed.

GLUCK

Well, I'm not stopping you. We can be in bed! *(Holding out a hand)* Come to bed, Connie, come to bed.

CONSTANCE

Just five more minutes. It's so rare for me to be up this late—not to have to think about going to the market in the morning, what flowers to buy, the next commission... let me enjoy it for a moment more...I want to imprint every memory of this holiday on my mind.

GLUCK

(Pouring them both some liqueur) We can stay up all night if that is what you desire. There are no rules here!

CONSTANCE

(Taking a glass) Thank you. And thank you for insisting that we dine here this evening, and for bringing me here and, well, for so much.

GLUCK

All our adventures will be together from now on.

CONSTANCE

(After a moment) Of course.

>   *Gluck kneels and embraces Constance.*

GLUCK

Did you know they've taken down the frames at the exhibition? They need the wood for salvage apparently!

CONSTANCE

Such beauty, gone in a few moments. It's a sign of the times.

GLUCK

In what way?

CONSTANCE

The economy of course.

GLUCK

Economy! I never think of it. You?

CONSTANCE

(Laughing) Yes! Well, sometimes! I'm a shopkeeper after all. Shav is always telling me not to forget about the bread and butter jobs.

GLUCK

Is that what I am, a bread and butter job?

Constance laughs again and drinks more liqueur.

There will be other exhibitions. Thanks to you and Syrie, but chiefly thanks to you, I really feel as if I've... made a start at last, carved a little niche for myself—

CONSTANCE

Oh more than that! The reviews! My celebrated artist, painting my flowers, flowers that I have done. Better than any photograph. I couldn't be happier. I shall use them in the next flower book I write, once the cookery book is out of the way.

Please, never forget those reviews, and the pleasure your work brought. And continues to bring. *(She presses Gluck's hand to her face.)* And not only to me, darling Gluck, to so many of us.

GLUCK

(Kissing the hand) Well, perhaps, but changing people's perception of art is a slow process—you yourself know that. I paint and I paint but still I wonder if I'm getting my message across.

CONSTANCE

We are so lucky to have this, this connection through our work.

Gluck lies with her head in Constance's lap. Constance strokes Gluck's masculine crop.

GLUCK

Has Shav said any more about us?

CONSTANCE

Good heavens, no. Anyway, what is there to say?

GLUCK

Well, so many weekends away from home and now a holiday!

CONSTANCE

There is nothing to discuss. Anyway, he is busy with Val, going over the books again. *(Trying to make light)* They're counting the pennies.

GLUCK

That is because Mrs. Spry is so generous! *(A beat)* It won't affect—

CONSTANCE

Good heavens, no! Don't worry about that.

GLUCK

(A beat. Relieved) She's a strange cat.

CONSTANCE

Who? The third person in my marriage?

GLUCK

(Chuckling) Yes, she's sort of a counterirritant isn't she?

CONSTANCE

But if Val is that, then what or who is the main irritant?

GLUCK

Well, perhaps not for you, for me. Because she makes you so unhappy.

CONSTANCE

(A beat) I always know when he has been unfaithful—he is always very nice to me, very solicitous, which really isn't in his nature. Perhaps I should like her more, be thankful. Though he called me 'sweetypops' the other day on the telephone, so I knew she was lurking: 'sweetypops' is always a sign!

I suppose one is never happy.

GLUCK

I *suppose* if you accept that you are not a very nice person, life becomes so much easier.

CONSTANCE

(Shifts a little. Guarded) Oh I didn't say Shav wasn't a nice person— he is, he is, of course he is. I wouldn't be here without him. And these last months, well, what with us being abroad and time here, well I've rather left Val and Rosemary to their own devices. Val

chiefly, as Rosemary is occupied with the book. I really couldn't run things without her... But don't think for a moment that Shav is the main irritant in my life, please.

GLUCK

(Rises, and kneels beside Constance) Well, not in yours, perhaps... perhaps we all have to accept the fact that none of us can totally have another human being. *(Slightly petulantly)* Perhaps I should find someone of my own, a wife of my own? Then I could face Shav, equally, man to man.

CONSTANCE

Oh, Gluck, please let's not spoil tonight. Spoil what we have, when we have so much.

GLUCK

By ignoring all the... the counterirritants that buzz around us?

CONSTANCE

If you like, yes!

GLUCK

I don't think I can do that, Constance.

CONSTANCE

You need to bury all those ghastly things the Meteor said to you. That you were born crooked, that you are—

GLUCK

Please stop Connie! It's not to do with that—

CONSTANCE

Are you sure? I was reading that—

GLUCK

I can't bear it when I love you so much, and want you so much and yet I can't have you.

CONSTANCE

But you do have me!

GLUCK

Only in little bits, an affair of little pieces.

CONSTANCE

(Indulgently) The best bits. The finer pieces.

GLUCK

Petals, not the whole flower.

CONSTANCE

(Bursts out laughing) Oh, my darling, too lofty—perhaps if it was confined to paper, but not spoken!

> Pause. Gluck rises sulkily and lights a cigarette.

CONSTANCE *(cont.)*

(Rising and going to Gluck) I'm sorry, I shouldn't have laughed. It was a beautiful thing to say. But please understand that people will always remain two halves, even if they are one. You do see that?

GLUCK

They don't have to be.

CONSTANCE

It distresses me as much as you, that I can't—

GLUCK

I doubt it.

CONSTANCE

Oh, Gluck, please.

GLUCK

Can't or won't or don't know how to?

CONSTANCE

My situation is so different to your own.

GLUCK

It doesn't have to be. I thought you were like me.

CONSTANCE

No, I am not like you. No one is. How could they be?

GLUCK

You know what I mean. Or have I just made my way in, because things were not going well between you and Shav? Life is hard enough for people like us—

CONSTANCE

(Almost to herself) Like us?

GLUCK

(Her anger growing) Without making it even harder for ourselves. You make me feel like Val! It's despicable! Do you put up with her, because it gets him off your back, so you can be with me?

CONSTANCE

What an expression! I think you've had too much liqueur.

GLUCK

You don't want to satisfy his needs, the rights of your husband, fulfil your duties as a wife, so you put up with some poisonous little tart, because she can! *Is that it?*

CONSTANCE

How dare you!

> Constance turns and walks away. During the scene the sun has been very gradually coming up.

GLUCK

Where are you going?

CONSTANCE

Where I should have gone hours ago—to bed!

GLUCK

(Shouting after Constance) You always do this, you always walk away from things that matter!

> Constance stops. She turns, and going to Gluck, kisses her.

CONSTANCE

Please, let's not spoil the night. Here, see, I haven't walked away.

GLUCK

It already is spoiled. We've spoiled it. Cheapened it. This is what we will keep and remember from Cornwall. You can be next to me, in my arms in fact, but still walking away from me, still ignoring what is really going on.

CONSTANCE

Then let us right it now, this minute.

GLUCK

But don't you see what you are doing?

CONSTANCE

(Hurriedly) Your next set of work, my next book. Which flowers do you think you will paint? Will you add some colour? *(Trying to make light of the situation)* The influence of Syrie's white room can't last forever you know! *(A beat)* My love for you?

GLUCK

(Resignedly) Very well.

> They make to exit.

(Pausing) Nesta was saying I should paint more portraits.

CONSTANCE

(Warily) Nesta?

GLUCK

(Pleased) Nesta Obermeyer. You remember? Syrie introduced me to her at the exhibition. She's very influential. She wants to help with the selection for the next one. Wants me to paint her in fact.

CONSTANCE

I see.

GLUCK

(Turning and pouring herself another liqueur, brighter) Look, the dawn is almost breaking, and it's still so early. Shall we have another

drink? Perhaps you're right. Let's talk of other things. I feel so much better now. I feel as if I could talk all night...

Constance exits as Gluck makes the last speech. A door slams, off. Gluck turns.

Blackout. Music

FIFTEEN

Flower Decorations Ltd. is projected across the stage. Lights up, on another part of the stage, implying an office downstairs. It is late in the day, the shop has closed. Val, with her back to the audience, is practising a speech, as if into a mirror, as the lights come up. She holds a paper in one hand and a small nosegay in the other. For a moment it could almost be Constance. She wears her shop apron over a severe-looking suit. She is mid-lecture (referring to the notes on occasion) though with none of the charm and sparkle and naturalness that Constance brings to her talks.

VAL

Instead, please bear in mind the call of 'Try anything once!' If one fails then at least be aware that you tried. Don't let your prejudice about colour influence your choices, or more importantly the choices of Nature and what she has made readily available to you. If you don't particularly like orange, for instance, remember that by eliminating orange from all your floral work, over the year, it is you who misses out.

Shav enters and stands in the doorway—unheard by Val—he wears a coat over his suit, he has come to collect her.

Also don't forget to be aware of the size of container that you choose: as with everything, never 'over-vase' your materials!

SHAV

(From the doorway) Do you think you should be doing that?

VAL

(Startled. Cross) Christ! How long have you been standing there?

SHAV

Long enough.

VAL

(Defensively) The Horse asked me to.

SHAV

Whatever for?

VAL

She was concerned that Mrs. Spry wouldn't be available for her talk on the 22nd.

SHAV

That doesn't sound like Rosemary, or Connie for that matter.

VAL

Oh, doesn't it?

> *A beat. They look at each other.*

SHAV

Come on, I'll drive you home.

VAL

(Putting down the flowers, but keeping hold of the notes. She walks towards him, and past him) Very well. *(She exits.)*

> *He glances at the discarded nosegay, walks towards them, picks them up, smells them a moment, and puts them into a glass of water, on the table, nearby. Turns, flicks off the light and exits. Music*

SIXTEEN

Syrie Maugham's residence, Chelsea is projected across the stage. Music and lights up as a wireless newsreader announces the date that has been set for the coronation of the future Edward VIII. An indication of the white sitting room is presented once again, revealed from behind a curtain or screen, only this time the room has undergone a transformation and bears the mark of Syrie's time in India: the mixed effect, of overlapping styles, jars somewhat. Syrie, dressed in a fussy, wool suit and Indian bangles, rises to switch off the news programme. Tea things have been laid out and she picks up her cup and saucer and stands before her guest. Constance, dressed as in Scene Twelve, sits sipping tea.

SYRIE

(Clicking off the wireless) Well, my dear, there we have it!

CONSTANCE

(Sadly) Indeed.

SYRIE

Poor man to be at the hands of a pushy, grabby female. I can't think why he didn't stick to Thelma Furness or Freda, much more acceptable, and happy not to be the centre of attention, but this woman! My God, how I loathe common women!

CONSTANCE

They may be very much in love—have you never thought of that?

SYRIE

(Snapping) Well, of course I have, but he's going to be the King of England. One would hope love didn't enter into it. More cake, dear?

CONSTANCE

(Rising, smiling at the impossible Syrie) Thank you, no. I really should be somewhere else. It's just I had to call on a client and found myself in the area.

SYRIE

Yes, yes, you said. So where should you be?

CONSTANCE

(Looking at her watch) Well, back at the shop actually. Rosemary will be wondering where I've got to.

SYRIE

Still going from strength to strength I hear.

CONSTANCE

Well, we seem to be keeping our—

SYRIE

Not having seen you for an age I presumed you were either sinking or swimming.

CONSTANCE

As a matter of fact, we are run off our feet, but there is always the threat of competition, so I keep my eyes open.

SYRIE

Oh, my dear, one must, one must!

I'm glad it's all going so well, just don't take your eye off the ball, that's all. Some of us are still trying to find the next great innovation. My last was three years ago!

A beat. Constance sits.

CONSTANCE

You don't approve of my friendship with Gluck, do you? That's what you mean isn't it?

SYRIE

(Going to her) We are as close as two women can be, as you well know. We've always discussed things, you and I, so of course I've become concerned when I've heard rumours. Then when I hear that you're never at the shop — by the way, Valmer was most helpful when I needed to place an order, though her idea of a discount leaves much to be desired—well, darling, I am concerned that is all.

CONSTANCE

Do you feel threatened?

SYRIE

Good Lord, why should I feel threatened? Please don't take offence. My interest is purely in your interest, my dear.

CONSTANCE

But you don't approve?

SYRIE

To be frank, no. Well, it's not that I don't approve, I've always been broad-minded, always, and of course I turn a blind eye to all that—

CONSTANCE

All what?

SYRIE

It is just that a woman must always think of her business, that's all.

CONSTANCE

But you were so complimentary to begin with, so helpful... How interested were you?

SYRIE

My dear! I'm only helpful when there is something in it for me! That is the rule of business, you know that as well as I. Though you seem to have forgotten of late. And now I see that there isn't anything in it for me.

CONSTANCE

Is that what the friendship is based on? You scratch my back, I'll—

SYRIE

Such a vulgar expression!

CONSTANCE

Oh, don't become Emily Post and tell me how to behave! We are women of trade, you've just said that yourself, self-made women and if that is the only thing that links us, then so be it!

SYRIE

(*Grandly*) I must remember that, though I'm bound to forget it.

They look at each other, as if for the first time.

Alright! Very well, I will tell you. Yes, our friendship is based on the business we throw in the way of the other, and yes, when I first helped Gluck it was because I knew I could make some gain out of it, and I did.

CONSTANCE

So nothing is ever done because you merely like someone, want to help them, see them prosper?

SYRIE

Of course not! The White Room was three years ago, everything is white now. I want to be ahead of the pack, not trailing behind it. I've pickled so much furniture these last years there isn't anything left. The flea markets of the South of France are a desert! I have to see who is new out there, who I can, can—

CONSTANCE

Feed off!

SYRIE

If you like! And when, my dear, you have been in the arts as long as I, and you've got the likes of Sybil Colefax and that viper de Woolf snapping at your heels, you too will gain a thicker skin of ruthlessness!

CONSTANCE

I don't see that my friendship with Gluck—

SYRIE

Such a stupid name. You do realize why she is so interested in you?

CONSTANCE

—that my friendship with Gluck, should have anything to do—

SYRIE

Is that all it is?

(*A beat*) Well? Is it? Remember I am quite au fait with the Glucks of this world!

CONSTANCE

I know.

SYRIE

So are you all happy? Shav and Val and you and Gluck, playing happy marriage but not with each other. Bouncing along like, like—

CONSTANCE

Like what, Syrie?

SYRIE

Of course, that's if one can call it marriage. You'll have to be careful, my dear. I want to protect you, as your friend. Imagine if that got out! The Spry Empire really would fall.

CONSTANCE

Well it won't, will it?

SYRIE

(*After a moment*) No. I won't, I won't let it.

> A beat. Syrie places a hand on Constance's.

My dear, people in the circles we revolve in might understand Gluck and yourself, but—

CONSTANCE

(*Moving away*) For the first time in my life, I really don't care.

SYRIE

Then you're an idiot! You must care! Just think what you are risking.

CONSTANCE

But what about what I might gain, have gained already! You don't know what she's like, Syrie, what we have together—it is like meeting the other part of yourself.

SYRIE

Oh, well, now you're just being silly. I thought all that nonsense wasn't for you. I thought we understood one another.

CONSTANCE

(Angrily) You make it sound depraved. It's more noble than that, a friendship of the truest kind.

Syrie begins to laugh archly.

Anyway, who are you to judge? A façade of a marriage, no, a sham of a marriage, worthy of one of his lesser novels—

SYRIE

People just won't understand it, accept it.

CONSTANCE

Let the opinion of others go hang!

SYRIE

You won't when they start patronising another florist!

CONSTANCE

And besides, what business is it of society's? Will they turn a blind eye for Somerset, but not for me?

SYRIE

(Ignoring the last remark, walking up and down, lighting a cigarette) And when I think of the sacrifices I have made to help. And you seem to be happy to see all you have built go up in smoke. Pouf! What would you do if this liaison were to collapse? Then where would you be? You would have risked your name as well as your marriage. And what of Shav in all this?

CONSTANCE

He is ably taken care of, as you well know!

SYRIE

Yes, but for how long? A woman can't behave like a man, even if she chooses to dress like one!

CONSTANCE

Then what are you suggesting? That I have it all as Somerset did? A wife to give his career an air of respectability, while he cavorts around the South of France with any boy that takes his fancy! If it works for a man then why not a woman?

SYRIE

(Rising) Too much, too far, you have gone too... I can't believe it of you. If I wasn't so fond of you, I would—

CONSTANCE

What? What? Tell me to get out?

SYRIE

(Beginning to 'sob') I can't believe it of you, can't believe you could be so callous. I'm only trying to help, to help you!

CONSTANCE

I must go.

SYRIE

Off to Hampstead?

CONSTANCE

You know very well where I'm going.

SYRIE

(Pause. Going towards a lamp) This isn't working here. Do you think it works here? Your mind is on other things, how could you? It's far too, too... white I suppose? I must bring some more colour into the room. Some more warmth... Connie?

CONSTANCE

Yes, the room could do with some more warmth.

Constance goes to the door to leave.

SYRIE

Thank you for the advice, my dear, and a word of warning in return. The world will keep spinning whether you are ready, or not!

CONSTANCE
I see.

SYRIE
I see? What does that mean? I see?

The two women look at each other. Then Constance exits.

SYRIE *(cont.)*
(Lighting a cigarette) Well, goodbye then. Mrs. Constance Spry.

(She picks up the telephone and dials.) Operator, Operator get me Flaxman 235. Thank you. *(A beat. She puffs on her cigarette.)* Nesta? Nesta, darling, it's Syrie, I need to speak to you, yes dear... about Gluck... I need your help...

The lights fade. Music fades in on Syrie as she speaks.

SEVENTEEN

Lights up. **The Studio, Bolton House, Hampstead** *is projected across the stage. An indication of Gluck's studio. Morning. Gluck in painter's smock, male attire beneath, is cleaning brushes; Constance, as she leaves the previous scene, removes her hat and jacket, enters the scene and in the course of it puts on new hat, jacket and gloves. These are set on stage. A half-finished portrait of a woman (Nesta) stands upon Gluck's easel, the face striking.*

CONSTANCE

(Looking at the painting before she prepares to leave) I see.

GLUCK

What do you mean "I see"?

CONSTANCE

I'm glad you've let me look at it at last.

GLUCK

I wasn't keeping it from you. I told you that before. I'm not happy with it, as yet, that was all.

CONSTANCE

I don't really know anything about painting do I? Only what I see, and flowers of course, but you seem to have moved on from flowers.

GLUCK

Oh, don't be like that, for heaven's sake.

CONSTANCE

I wasn't, I think it's very accomplished, you know how I feel about your work.

I should be going, I'm going to be late, I'm—

GLUCK

Goodbye, then. Call me, won't you?

CONSTANCE

—meeting Rosemary at the shop. We have to load up and get to Richmond! *(She laughs nervously. Uncomfortable)*

GLUCK

Oh, yes, you did say.

> *Constance makes to go. Then removes a shoe, wriggles her toes and puts it back on.*

GLUCK *(cont.)*
Constance.

CONSTANCE
Yes?

GLUCK

(Looking at the brushes she is cleaning) Last night.

CONSTANCE
Yes?

GLUCK

Well, I feel we said too much, said things we shouldn't have. Went too far, left no stone unturned...

CONSTANCE

(Quietly) And look what crawled out.

GLUCK

(Looking up) Connie!

CONSTANCE

It's true though isn't it? There was a time when telling each other everything was imperative to you, you demanded it. Yet now we seem to have lives shrouded from the other.

GLUCK

I can't wait forever, for something that can never be mine. You have to understand that. I have needs. I have to feel I'm investing in something, that I have a future.

CONSTANCE

As I invested in you?

GLUCK

That isn't fair.

CONSTANCE

I thought others saw to your needs, but that you would come back to me. I never minded. I thought— *(Becoming upset)* I'm so confused, I don't know. I just don't know, Gluck. When I'm doing the flowers, there is no doubt, no thought of what I should do. Everything is instinctive, but in life it is all such a muddle at the moment... I suppose I need to think things through more: it has always been a snag of mine not to.

GLUCK

(Wanting to go to Constance, but resisting) You have Shav. You always said he was your guide.

CONSTANCE

But that's different! How can you compare it?

GLUCK

I found such solace with you once. You were always there.

CONSTANCE

Is that what you want me to be, though? Your wife, as I am Shav's wife, and then you could have Nesta as your mistress! Is that it? You really would be living life as a man if you think you can pull that one off! Your journey complete, by becoming the thing you most despise. A man!

GLUCK

(Contained anger) I can't think why you keep harking back to Nesta. What harm has the woman done you? You hardly know her.

CONSTANCE

I'm growing to know her, through you. Another married woman, that will satisfy you for a while, until you crave a future with her.

GLUCK

Please stop, Connie. You don't know what you are saying.

CONSTANCE

Or will she give up her husband? Or is her allowance dependent upon him?

GLUCK

I said shut up!

> She smashes down her palette, causing Constance to start.

GLUCK (cont.)

You can't have expected things to go on as they were.

CONSTANCE

That is what Syrie said.

GLUCK

Of course! Syrie.

This is all so unlike you. You know, I'm afraid you're not well.

CONSTANCE

Then who else is it? Who else stands before you if it isn't me? Hmm? No one, I have to disappoint you, no one, certainly nobody new and exciting, no one but your tired, old Connie of whom you seem to have tired also. The person you once wanted as your wife.

GLUCK

Oh Connie, it all comes back to Nesta again. I'm beginning to think you have a passion for her yourself!

CONSTANCE

I don't, but you do.

GLUCK

Nesta Obermyer is a very influential patron of the arts. She merely wants to help me, introduce me to people, help with the next exhibition. You know this. It was a commission I couldn't refuse.

CONSTANCE

Nesta towers over me, in every way, in all her accomplishments. She is a bold brushstroke of a woman, and I am not. Don't you see that? Don't you see how that makes me feel?

GLUCK

I think you underestimate yourself, your achievements. If I didn't know you better I would say you were being rather ridiculous.

CONSTANCE

Ridiculous! I think at last I have gained a sense of perspective, and I see I have been... have been not addressing things in my life, my work chiefly, that I should have, Gluck. I really should have.

GLUCK

Well, perhaps it is time to address those things. I'm sure you can't mean your marriage, though, you must mean the business—that always seems takes a precedent.

CONSTANCE

I see I was something of a stepping stone for you, and it isn't a nice feeling. *(She breaks down again.)*

GLUCK

Run along then, don't let me keep you from your flower vases. Go and find the next big thing you and Syrie always claim you're searching for.

CONSTANCE

And I shall leave you to your portrait.

GLUCK

Please don't be so acid! There have always been others, you know that. Encouraged it even!

CONSTANCE

(Blowing her nose) This time it is different.

GLUCK

You've been talking to the white witch again haven't you? Nesta knows her too. Every word is laced with her venom!

CONSTANCE

It wasn't so many years ago you were begging me to meet her, clamouring to get an introduction to the famous Mrs. Maugham, sniff around her influential address book! Although now it seems you have found a patron with a weightier tome than even Syrie and I combined could have produced!

GLUCK

Shut up! Shut up! These are not your words, simply not your phrases.

CONSTANCE

Perhaps not, but they will do. *(Turning from her)* I need to get to the shop. *(A pause as she looks at her reflection and fastens on her hat. Calmly)* You have treated me badly, Gluck. It wasn't a kind way to treat a friend.

GLUCK

Stop being such a snob. I thought you understood the world I introduced you to and how it operates.

CONSTANCE

It would seem I haven't taken to it as easily as you have to mine.

> *Constance looks at her for a moment, then picks up her bag and briefcase and exits. Gluck sighs irritably and turns to the light. She pauses, looking into it, before collecting up her painting equipment and exiting. Lights fade. Music*

EIGHTEEN

The Ladies Guild of Florists is projected across the screen. Music fades. Floral images in the vein of Constance's work are shown as if by slides. Dust particles fill the air and the noise of the projector buzzes. The images are in black and white. Constance's voice accompanies these: 'A pond of water-lilies, flag irises, alliums, garden lilac, rhododendron bushes, cabbage leaves' etc. After a little time has elapsed Constance, dressed as before, steps forward and up on to the platform to interrupt the slide show as it shows several images of roses. The images continue across her body. She shields her eyes. Some noise from her implied audience.

CONSTANCE

(A little flustered) Thank you, thank you so very much. Oh yes, well, if we could just stop the pictures coming for a moment... could we? Oh, thank you, yes, that's better, and a little light? *(The dim light slightly brightens.)* Thank you. Yes, right, well, roses, glorious roses of June. So much to say about them, that they really deserve a talk of their own, but there isn't time for that today. *(Speaking quickly)* Though don't be tempted to disregard other flowers in favour of the rose. Think beyond your rose gardens, ladies, think beyond your flower beds in fact: hedgerows, the fields, even the vegetable patch can contain gems that can be exploited and admired!

Be brave! Make bold, radical decisions as to what you display your flowers in! Just think what is happening in modern design at the moment. The Shakespeare Memorial Theatre, built and designed by a woman; the new Lambeth Bridge, also by a woman. And opened by our dear king. Artists! Dame Laura Knight! Take inspiration from all around you and incorporate that into your designs! *(A satisfied beat)* And now back to the slides. *(She goes to leave the podium and then remembers. But the slides by this time have continued.)* Ah yes, roses! I was going to say something uplifting about roses, wasn't I? *(Looking at the pictures as she stands in front of the images, her audience enraptured. Images of roses illustrate her talk.)* Not difficult, as some of you by now will know. Never, has the rose not been able to lift me, and I hope they have the same effect on you. Their names alone have a note of music and mystery about them: Damask, Centifolia, Bourbon, Hebe's Lip, Village Maid, Tricolor de Flandre, Rosa Mundi, Black Moss, Double de Coubert and perhaps the most perfect of all: the Alba rose. They make me want to compose, or at least be gifted enough to paint. *(She delves into a pocket, retrieves a handkerchief and dabs at her brow. The image of the 'Alba' flowers that Constance will soon arrange for Gluck appears. Constance reacts momentarily to it, then quickly.)* Ah, now here are some flowers, or rather a display of flowers that I was commissioned to arrange some time ago for a client... a client who wished to paint them. *(To the projectionist)* I was talking about the Alba rose, has there been some sort of mix up? *(The slide jams and we hear the click of the machine trying to show the next image. To her audience again, uncomfortable)* An all white commission that was indeed painted, that was—oh dear, can we move on to the next slide? Or at least back to the roses. *(The slides continues to jam, the noise increasing as they pile up. She becomes more anxious, looking into the darkness in front of her, the noise intensifies. She mops her brow with a handkerchief.)* Please can we move on? I had no idea that display was even amongst these slides. Can we move on? It shouldn't be there. *(With weight) It shouldn't be there!*

    Blackout. Music

NINETEEN

Flower Decorations Ltd. is projected across the stage, along with images of the shop once again. Lights up, music fades. Rosemary and Val, wearing skirts and light pullovers and their shop aprons/housecoats, are at work on a large floral and pedestal display, consisting of cow parsley, herbs and various late spring/early summer foliage and blossom. About them are buckets of branches and lime: the finished effect will be a green and white arrangement. A small reception desk, at the rear of the shop, bears a telephone. It is early morning. As the scene progresses, the light increases. As the music fades it is apparent the two women are mid conversation...

ROSEMARY

One would hope it wouldn't happen, but it's difficult to tell isn't it?

VAL

It won't. The Prime Minister won't let it.

ROSEMARY

You think?

VAL

Of course, we can't go through all that again. Besides we've got the King to sort out first! You shouldn't take as gospel all the rubbish you hear on the wireless.

Trust me.

Rosemary attempts a smile. They work for a moment more in silence. Putting the display together, Rosemary doing the more artistic tasks, Val the more technical. Branches are fastened into position with chicken wire. Val strips some leaves from a branch.

VAL

Reminds me of when I first started! Great buckets of lime and all the leaves had to be stripped off. I thought she'd gone mad!

ROSEMARY

But you soon realized she hadn't. I've never known Connie wrong about anything yet.

VAL

Haven't you?

ROSEMARY

No, I haven't.

Do you think those buds will be opening yet?

VAL

I'll have a look in a moment. They really aren't ready, but I knew we needed them and Shav was with me, so it seemed too opportune not to pick them. The hot water will bring them out.

ROSEMARY

Was this at Park Gate?

VAL

(Cautiously) Yes, I had a lot of receipts to go over with Shav, and as Connie was away again... working on the book with you, wasn't she?

ROSEMARY

(Lying) Yes, yes, that's right.

 A beat.

VAL

I think those flower paintings of Gluck's rather lumpish, don't you?

ROSEMARY

Well, they aren't to my taste particularly, but I wouldn't exactly call them lumpish. And don't let Connie hear you say that.

VAL

As if I would! Anyway, she's on the telephone planning her week apparently, calling Hampstead I presume—

ROSEMARY

(Warning) Val!

VAL

And then she's buying the buns for the girls, I presume it will be another late one tonight. I ask you! In at five and—

ROSEMARY

And we are happy to do it. I can't think of any other way I'd like to spend my time.

VAL

No?

ROSEMARY

No!

> They work.

VAL

By the way, how is the book coming along?

ROSEMARY

Slowly, I'm afraid, Connie has been so busy of late... I've managed a lot of it myself but we really do need to put our heads together.

VAL

Yes, she has been busy hasn't she? Well, I'm sure it will be a huge success.

ROSEMARY

(Laughing) It isn't even finished yet, it may never happen.

VAL

It will, if Mrs. Spry is behind it.

ROSEMARY

What do you say that?

VAL

She gets what she wants doesn't she? She makes things happen.

ROSEMARY

(Stops) Yes, yes I suppose she does. Thank goodness. *(A beat)* She does appreciate you, you know. She does realize all you do for her.

VAL

Oh, I know that. I know my worth. Connie would have had a pretty difficult time if it wasn't for me taking care of things.

> *A door bangs off. They both look towards it, then quickly get on with their tasks. Constance enters wearing a smart summer suit and hat and carrying a large bag of buns. She puts these down and removes her hat and puts an apron/overall on as she talks.*

CONSTANCE

(She does things even faster than usual and seems somewhat agitated.) Well, well, they are coming along. Suitable, suitable! And lovely warm buns for the girls.

ROSEMARY

We still have to add the blossom that Val—

CONSTANCE

Oh, yes. Clever Val, spotting them when you did. What it really needs is some colour, don't you think?

VAL

The order was for white and green, Connie.

CONSTANCE

I know, I know, but I'm just becoming so tired of it. Aren't you?

ROSEMARY

Well, it does seem to have had its day somewhat.

VAL

Don't let the old bag Maugham hear you say that!

ROSEMARY

Val, really!

CONSTANCE

(Adjusting some of their work with speed) Oh, if only I had a third hand, darling. *(To Val)* Pass me one stem more. *(She inserts another. To Rosemary)* You don't mind, do you?

ROSEMARY

No, no, certainly not.

CONSTANCE

(To Val) There now, finish that.

VAL

What it really needs is something like Monkshood.

ROSEMARY

Or why not Hogweed or Deadly Nightshade!

CONSTANCE

(Chuckling) Now, now, ladies. But Val has a point: poisonous or not, a blast of colour would be most suitable. But alas, we must give them what they have asked for. Now, come along, let's have no more nonsense, and lots of speed. And aren't there some flowers back from the Douglas-Scott ball?

ROSEMARY

I think so, yes.

CONSTANCE

Well, shove those in!

VAL

But they have already been used.

ROSEMARY

(To Constance) Are you alright my dear?

> *Constance smile and nods, placing her hand on Rosemary's arm reassuringly.*

CONSTANCE

(To Val. Twinkling) Well, use them again, darling. You do want us to get our money's worth, don't you?

VAL

And how will that be achieved?

CONSTANCE

Because I presume you will charge them to this account as well as the last.

VAL

Very well. *(Collecting the buns)* I'll take these through to the girls.

CONSTANCE

(Making eye contact with Rosemary) Thank you, dear. They'll appreciate that.

> *Val makes for the door. Constance begins to assemble the branches for the next display, as Rosemary finishes off the first. The telephone rings.*

CONSTANCE *(cont.)*

Val, could you get that?

VAL

(Picking up the telephone) Flower Decorations, good morning... Yes, she is here. Who is speaking, please?... Just a moment and I will put her on, please hold... Oh?

> *Constance dries her hands in her apron and moves towards the telephone. She pauses. Rosemary looks up.*

VAL *(cont.)*

Oh...Very well. I can pass on the message, of course I can... But she is just here if you wish to... Very well, I will tell her... Thank you, Good morning. *(She replaces the receiver and gets up from the desk, and comes towards Constance.)*

CONSTANCE

And who was it? *(Amused)* Who didn't want to speak to me?

VAL

It was Miss Gluck's secretary.

CONSTANCE

You mean Gluck.

VAL

Yes, sorry, it was Gluck's secretary.

CONSTANCE

But I've just spoken to her—

VAL

To say that she can't put you up on Thursday and Friday as you hoped.

CONSTANCE

(A beat. Thinking) How strange. The poor woman must have made a mistake. I wasn't going to stay there on those days.

ROSEMARY

(Sensing that something is not right) Maybe she turned the wrong page over in the diary. I'm forever doing that myself.

VAL

I didn't even know she had a secretary—She is grand!

ROSEMARY

Sshh, Val!

CONSTANCE

No, it's alright, Rosemary, and yes, she does have a secretary now...

Pause, they look at Constance, who seems lost in thought.

ROSEMARY

Are you sure you're alright, dear?

CONSTANCE

Well, that's that then. *(Coming to her senses)* Yes, quite sure, thank you. It's of no consequence. It was something and nothing. Something and nothing. *(A beat. She looks at the finished display that Rosemary has been working on.)* You know, darling, Val is quite right: they do need Monkshood, a loud explosion of them!

I saw some out the back. Go and fetch them, Val.

VAL

Very well. *(She exits.)*

ROSEMARY

But the order states specifically white and green, Connie.

CONSTANCE

(Laughing and crying at the same time) Well, we will just have to convince them otherwise!

You know what this means, don't you, Rosemary? You knew things were going badly. You know what this means!

Constance begins to make space in the finished arrangements, with terrific speed and vigour, almost hysterically, pulling out cow parsley etc. as the lights fade. Rosemary looks on, concerned, not knowing what to do.

ROSEMARY

Oh, Constance. I'm so sorry, so very sorry.

Constance stops what she is doing and falls into Rosemary's arms sobbing.

Fade to black. Music

TWENTY

Music fades. Lights gradually up. Flower Decorations Ltd. at night. Constance is still toiling away busily, as she completes one of the pedestal arrangements, working the Monkshood into the display. She is dressed as before, though she wears gloves, and her appearance shows what a busy day she has had, even if she does not. She has been crying. She works alone, her back to us. After a moment Shav's figure appears at the back of the shop. He is dressed in his dinner jacket. Constance doesn't notice him at first. He carries a parcel: a dressmaker's box/parcel.

CONSTANCE

Shav! Good heavens, whatever are you doing here?

SHAV

(Coming to her) Have you seen the time?

CONSTANCE

(Looking at her watch) Oh, Shav, well I—who would have thought it! It only seemed a moment ago Rosemary said 'Goodnight' to me.

SHAV

Yes, I've just been talking to Rosemary, she looks done in. *(A beat)* I was on my way home from the club, I saw lights were still on...

CONSTANCE

(Still working) Nothing new about that!

SHAV

Well, I just felt I wanted to poke my head round the door, see if it *was* you here.

CONSTANCE

(To herself. Flatly) That it was me?

SHAV

Take you home.

CONSTANCE

I've a lot to catch up on, that's why I stayed. So much to catch up on. And I'm afraid yet more to do.

SHAV

But not tonight. I want you home tonight.

> *Pause. They look at each other, understanding the other.*

CONSTANCE

(Sincerely) Thank you.

> *She removes her apron/overall and prepares herself to leave the premises.*

SHAV

Also, Connie, I think we should have a talk about things, Rosemary mentioned something, but I really think we need to—

CONSTANCE

(Taking note of the parcel for the first time) What have you got there?

A talk? What about?

SHAV

It was waiting for you on the desk upstairs, had your name addressed on it, thought you must have wanted to take it home.

> *She takes the parcel from him.*

SHAV *(cont.)*

Thought you must have ordered yourself a frock or something.

CONSTANCE

No, no, of course I haven't.

> *She unties the string on the parcel and opens the box, ravelling the string around her fingers. She removes a sheet of tissue paper and pulls out a night gown. As she holds it up a toothbrush falls out of its folds. Shav stoops and picks it up, handing it to her.*

SHAV

Bought yourself a nightie have you? And a toothbrush? I don't understand? Connie?

CONSTANCE

(After a moment) I do.

SHAV

Then what is it? You planning on going away? *(He chuckles, embarrassed.)*

CONSTANCE

They're mine. My toothbrush, my... nightie.

SHAV

I don't understand then.

CONSTANCE

They've been returned to me.

SHAV

Returned?

CONSTANCE

(A beat) Gluck sent them. *She* returned them to me.

SHAV

Well, why would she do that? *(A beat)* Oh. Oh, I see.

She pulls a chair up, sits a moment, kicking off her shoes, and stares out front.

CONSTANCE

I'm always rushing to the next thing, aren't I?

SHAV

And you're famous for it, Connie.

CONSTANCE

Well, I think I've finally ground to a halt.

SHAV

Not Connie, certainly not!

CONSTANCE

It's all over. It's all over with Gluck.

SHAV

I see.

CONSTANCE

I suppose I've had something of an adventure, haven't I?

SHAV

Oh, Connie. *(Drawing up another chair and sitting next to her and taking her hand tenderly)* I should say you probably have.

CONSTANCE

And now I need to return to what I was before. I have to. *(A beat)* You never cared for her, did you?

SHAV

Truth be told, no, I didn't. I didn't understand her.

CONSTANCE

I thought I did. *(She begins to weep.)* I feel such a fool. What if it got out? I couldn't bear it, just couldn't bear it if it got out!

SHAV

(Soothingly) Who will ever find out?

CONSTANCE

(Looking at him) I've neglected you also, haven't I? As well as the business. I've not been there when I—

SHAV

(He hands her his handkerchief.) There may have been times when I might have preferred my wife to have merely done the flowers for parties for her friends, or not taken up with lady painters from Hampstead, but I'm immensely proud of your achievements, Connie, I truly am. The next big thing is always around the corner for you. You're not a fool.

CONSTANCE

(Dabbing her eyes, she takes his hand) When I was a teacher, I recall a little girl being brought before me for stealing a shilling. A pathetic slip of a girl. And when I asked her why she had done it, what had prompted her to commit such a terrible crime, she had told me that she had bought coloured paper flowers with it, because they were so pretty. She craved some beauty in her otherwise dreary, backwater life. And I've never forgotten that incident.

I wanted beauty, hated dreary, and I have beauty every day of my life, just by looking at a flower.

But I also wanted adventure... and now adventure I have had.

SHAV

We all crave that, Connie, of course we do.

CONSTANCE

Val?

SHAV

(A beat) Yes.

CONSTANCE

I don't mind. I really don't.

SHAV

What is it you're always saying? Beware of stylizing, accept no rules, flowers can be your paintbox. Can't that be true of life also?

> *She looks at him a moment and then takes his face in her hands.*

CONSTANCE

I was going to say, it is times like these that I see why I married you, Shav. Only I haven't married you!

SHAV

(Overlapping) Only you haven't married me!

> *They kiss.*

Now, I think we should get home.

> *They rise to leave.*

CONSTANCE

I've got the market in the morning—

SHAV

That's right, you have. And the next big thing to find!

CONSTANCE

(Tidying herself and putting her shoes back on, blowing her nose.) I've been thinking about that.

SHAV

(Amused) Oh, yes?

CONSTANCE

I know what we'll do next season!

> *They begin to exit, walking upstage.*

Cut flowers! We should sell cut flowers as well as all the design commissions. That way anyone can just walk in off the street and purchase a bunch, take them home and design them for themselves.

SHAV

Don't you think that might put us out of business? People doing their own flowers?

CONSTANCE

(*Growing animated*) Not at all, I think it could be the way forward for floristry.

SHAV

Not floristry, my dear, flower decoration. Floristry is a trade.

She takes his arm. They exit.

CONSTANCE

Now what is it you wanted to talk to me about?

SHAV

(*A beat*) Oh, nothing, Connie, it doesn't matter now.

Music fades up and the lights fade in. The couple link arms and make their way upstage. Constance flicks off light switches and one by one the lights go out over the flower arrangements. The lights fade, the couple disappear. One large coloured arrangement remains, before blackout.

The End

Lightning Source UK Ltd.
Milton Keynes UK
UKOW04f1332100913

216924UK00001B/1/P